Praise for

Three Minutes with God

....

"Grounded in the wisdom of Holy Scripture, the saints, and a
lifetime of priestly ministry, Monsignor Frank Bognanno's *Three
Minutes with God* is both accessible and deep in its reflections on
the human experience and encounter with God in daily life."
—JASON KURTH,
chancellor of the Diocese of Des Moines

"This book is a double treat. Not only do you get to spend three
minutes with God on each and every page, you get to spend
time with Monsignor Frank Bognanno. Father Frank's wisdom,
compassion, humor and peaceful presence permeate each page.
He has been a source of comfort and strength to me and to many
of my cancer patients who have had the opportunity to have him
accompany them on their journey."
—RICHARD L. DEMING, MD,
medical director of MercyOne Cancer Center and
founder of Above + Beyond Cancer

"Do you need to be encouraged? Do you need to be strengthened? Do you need to know God better? Do you need to feel God's love? Monsignor Bognanno is enthusiastic and joyful as he presents the Word in brief, understandable morsels that encourage, strengthen, and teach about God and His love for us. I found myself leaning in to Monsignor Bognanno's practical, easy to implement wisdom and ideas for daily living. With each page I was motivated to turn to the next. What a great book for daily prayer and meditation!"

—CHRIS MAGRUDER,
founder and chairman of The Veil Removed

Three Minutes with God

Reflections and Prayers to Encourage, Inspire, and Motivate

MONSIGNOR FRANK BOGNANNO

franciscan
media®
Cincinnati, Ohio

I dedicate this book to...

My parents, Michael and Iola Bognanno, whose wisdom and faith guided my academic, spiritual, and moral development by providing me with twelve years of Catholic school education;

My brother Mario and his wife, Peggy, and my sister Patty James and her husband, Joseph, whose love and encouragement strengthened my priestly ministry over the past five decades;

My cousin Paul and his wife, Teri, who have assisted me in many special ways over the years, and to all of my relatives, their families, and to my friends.

Scripture quotations are taken from the *New Revised Standard Version Bible, Catholic Edition*, copyright 1989, Division of Christian Education of the National Council of the Churches of Christ in the United States of America. Used by permission. All rights reserved.

Library of Congress Control Number: 2022943765

Cover and book design by Mark Sullivan
Copyright ©2022 by Frank Bognanno. All rights reserved.
ISBN 978-1-63253-426-2

Published by Franciscan Media
28 W. Liberty Street
Cincinnati, OH 45202-6498
www.FranciscanMedia.org

Printed in the United States of America

Contents

Foreword

....

The prophet Isaiah conveys God's message that his servant will be like a "polished arrow," hidden in his quiver until being deployed to do God's work (see Isaiah 49:2). The book you hold before you is such a quiver, filled with the penetrating reflections and insights composed by Monsignor Frank E. Bognanno and offered for our spiritual enrichment. As he comments upon Mark 9:24, "Faith is based on the various truths God shares with us, especially the fact that God's love is all present each moment and is unconditional." Monsignor's reflections illuminate truths that spring not only from Sacred Scripture, but from the rich intellectual and spiritual resources of Catholic tradition in which he is well steeped—all with an economy of words that make his insights eminently accessible and user-friendly.

The "arrows" he sets before us emerge from nearly six decades of priestly service in which he has enabled God's Word to reveal and heal human hearts and has strengthened the hope of the faithful in the Diocese of Des Moines, and all those within broadcast range of his daily messages. Here his own heart is on display: a heart that is aflame with love for the Eucharistic Jesus and for the entire Body of Christ's Church. His ministry has extended far beyond central Iowa to the people of various regions and continents in which he has been an ambassador of good will and the joy of the Gospel.

He is, with all due respect and affection, a "spiritual entrepreneur" who is not afraid to enlist the means and media at his disposal to announce Jesus Christ and to enlist others in support of this sacred mission. This book is one more initiative in this regard; may it draw readers to ponder the things that are above and to follow the trajectory of its arrows to the far reaches of heaven.

—Most Reverend William M. Joensen, Ph.D.
Bishop of Des Moines
Holy Week 2022

Preface

Father, I abandon myself into your hands, do with me what you will. Whatever you may do I thank you. I am ready for all, I accept all. Let only your will be done in me and in all your creatures. I wish no more than this, O Lord. Into your hands I commend my life. I offer it to you with all the love of my heart. For I love you. Lord, and so need to give myself, to surrender myself into your hands with out reserve and with boundless confidence, for you are my Father. Amen —St. Charles de Foucauld

....

This book is a testimony to one of my most basic and cherished beliefs—the guiding hand of Divine Providence. It all began with a step-in-faith by Carolyn Lawrence some twenty-five years ago while I was pastor of St. Augustine parish in Des Moines, Iowa. She fell in love with the history and teachings of the Catholic Church. Her husband joined her on her journey, and both became active members.

A few years later in her position at a local television station, Carolyn invited me to produce one-minute "Thought of the Day" television spots. God's hand was at work. I was able to get the financial support needed for both the production and airing of the programs. Since 2015, we have produced over 250 programs viewed each weekday on WHO-TV (NBC) Channel 13 in Des Moines.

But the hand of Providence did not rest. With so many scripts available, the idea occurred to us to make a book of them. I shared the idea with one of my nieces, Patty Jo Crawford, Director of Marketing at Franciscan Media, and she brought the proposal to the rest of the team. The rest is history. The hand of God. Divine Providence. Here is the book!

The reflections can be read cover to cover or in any order. Browse the table of contents and find a reflection title that meets your need or stirs your curiosity on any given day, or open the book at random during your daily prayer time. If you don't already have a daily prayer time, use this book to begin that habit.

—Monsignor Frank Bognanno

Part One

ENCOURAGEMENT

Rise Up!

"When I fall, I shall rise; when I sit in darkness, the Lord
will be a light to me."—MICAH 7:8

A wise and spiritual woman once wrote to me her thoughts on
something we all experience: failure in trying to become better
or more virtuous. She wrote: "Holiness or virtue does not consist
in so rising above failings that we never fail. In fact, it consists in
failing and failing often—but each time, with each failure, rising up
quickly and asking forgiveness of God and others and all the while
maintaining our peace of heart." That is real virtue; that is true holiness of soul. Rising up immediately after a failure. Perseverance!

Prayer

When I fall, Lord, help me back up immediately. Amen.

The Unsearchable Ways of God

"I am about to do a new thing; now it springs forth,
do you not perceive it?"—ISAIAH 43:19

God is a God of surprises. He's a God of newness. Study the Hebrew Scriptures and the New Testament. Noah, mocked by all for building an ark on dry land, was saved. Moses uprooted the Jewish people in Egypt and led them to a new land. This was God's unfathomable plan brought into the lives of his people. This was newness God brought into their lives. Whenever God reveals himself, he brings newness. In the beginning, as with Noah and Moses, openness to God demands our trust in him. Let God surprise you! Accept the new thing he wants to do in your life. What is the step of trust God wants you to take?

Prayer

O God, my Strength, I place my trust in you. You never forsake those who seek you. Amen.

Prayer in Suffering

"In the day of my trouble I call on you, for you
will answer me."—Psalm 86:7

....

We go through periods of suffering during our life. The suffering
might be physical, emotional, or relational. It might be short-term
or long-term. But perhaps it's really an invitation to turn our minds
and hearts to God. It's an invitation to open ourselves to God's
unconditional love for us personally. The best prayer is short but
powerful. It's a one-word prayer: "Help!" Yes, just "Help!" Pray it
with peace, calm, and trust. Then wait in silence and watch for God's
response. Add on other words if you want. Help is on the way.

Prayer

Lord, help me to see that my suffering is often a call to pray. Amen.

Let God Reign

"Be strong and courageous; do not be frightened or dismayed, for the Lord your God is with you wherever you go."—JOSHUA 1:9

We are not on a lonely journey, all alone on a long road. Our loving Father never takes his eyes off us. We all are subject to feelings of fear and anxiety. All the great saints repeatedly tell us, "Don't let those negative feelings control you." It's damaging to the good that God has created in you. It paralyzes your potential and cripples your natural gifts and talents. How do you thrust those feelings away? Know the truth! There is another who loves you as you are and cares deeply about your situation. Your loving, ever-present, ever-caring Heavenly Father is only a breath away.

Jesus tells us to pray always—"cry to [God] day and night" (Luke 18:7). We can all do that. God is holding you and me by the hand along the path he has marked out for us. Simply whisper a simple prayer—"Lord, help me," or "Thanks, Lord"—to let God know you're holding his hand, too. With any short, spontaneous prayer, we reach out to grasp God, and God lovingly grasps us.

Prayer

Lord, show me that I am never alone on my life's journey. I abandon myself into your hands. Amen.

Do Not Worry

"So do not worry about tomorrow, for tomorrow will
bring worries of its own."—MATTHEW 6:34

I recently saw a poster that read, "Worry is the misuse of the imagination." Things seldom happen as we expect. Most of our fears turn out to be our imaginings. The difficulties we anticipated become very simple in reality. The real difficulties are often the things we never anticipated. It's better to accept things as they come, one after another, trusting that we will have the grace to deal with them at the right time. The best way to prepare for the future is to put our hearts in the present. Projecting into the future cuts us off from reality and saps our energy. St. Francis de Sales counseled:

Do not look forward to what may happen tomorrow; the same everlasting Father who cared for you today will take care of you tomorrow and every day. Either He will shield you from suffering, or He will give you unfailing strength to bear it. Be at peace, then. Put aside all anxious thoughts and imaginations and say continually: "The Lord is my strength and my shield; My heart has trusted in Him and I am being helped. He is not only with me, but in me and I am in Him."

Prayer

Lord, you are closer to me than I am to myself. Help me to stay with you in the present moment. Amen.

Patience with Oneself

"Rejoice in hope, be patient in suffering,
persevere in prayer."—ROMANS 12:12

Of the hundreds of canonized saints in the Church, one of the most practical was the seventeenth-century French bishop Francis de Sales. He thought that what we need is a cup of understanding, a barrel of love, and an ocean of patience. He went on to say: "Have patience with all things...but first, be patient with yourself; never confuse your mistakes with your value as a human being. You are a perfectly valuable, creative, worthwhile person simply because you exist. And no amount of triumph or tribulation can ever change that."

Treasure the truth of this saint's wise words. Your value as a person never changes. That's the truth! Be patient with yourself as you live into God's unfolding plan for your life.

Prayer

Lord, help me to love myself with the same love you have for me. Amen.

Renew Your Strength

"I can do all things through him who
strengthens me."—Philippians 4:13

How can you or I hasten through the day today and not grow
weary? How can we go through life's paces and not grow tired? We
find the answer in Isaiah 40:30–31:

Even youths will faint and be weary,

and the young will fall exhausted;

but those who wait for the Lord shall renew their strength,

they shall mount up with wings like eagles;

they shall run and not be weary, they shall walk and not faint.

Start each morning and end each evening with a prayer of trust in
the Father's love. You will find God's helping hand in each step.
That trust will help you to walk and not stumble, to run and not
grow weary.

Prayer

Lord, I trust your love for me—increase that grace of trust. Amen.

God Alone

"Cast all your anxiety on him, because he
cares for you."—1 PETER 5:7

....

In times of stress and difficulty, these words of wisdom from St.
Teresa of Avila can bring deep peace to our souls:

Let nothing disturb you;

Let nothing make you afraid;

All things are passing;

God alone is changeless;

Patience gains all things;

Whoever has God wants nothing;

God alone suffices.

Think about that as you live out this day. God alone is all we
really need.

Prayer

Lord, show me that you are enough. Amen.

Accept Your Weakness

"Whenever I am weak, then I am strong."
—2 CORINTHIANS 12:10

....

Jesus began his preaching by giving us the eight Beatitudes. The very first one is "Blessed are the poor in spirit, for theirs is the kingdom of heaven" (Matthew 5:3). What does it mean to be "poor in spirit"? It simply means "Blessed are those who know their need for God." They realize they are weak and finite, and they know that God's love is the infinite source of strength for them each day.

If you feel "poor in spirit," your human soul probably feels empty; maybe that's good. Maybe now there is room for a deeper relationship with God. St. Francis of Assisi repeatedly prayed, "Who are you, God, and who am I?" If we make room for this prayer in our poverty of spirit, we make room for the great truth of life: God is love, and we are his beloved.

Jesus clearly tells us that God loves us not in spite of our weakness, but *because* of our weakness. Being "poor in spirit," we become blessed because our spiritual poverty opens us up to true riches, God's riches. When you feel poor in spirit, thank God, for you are open at that moment to his mercy, grace, and joy. Yes, the kingdom of heaven is yours!

Prayer

Lord, help me to realize that my weaknesses are open doors for you. Amen.

Simply Ask

"Ask, and it will be given to you; search, and you will find."
—MATTHEW 7:7

A Scripture passage from the prophet Isaiah gives us great hope: "I was ready to be sought out by those who did not ask" (Isaiah 65:1). The Jewish people were in a difficult situation at the time of Isaiah. Their God, our God, who loved them so much, was waiting to help them, waiting for their prayer request. But they did not pray. Why? Perhaps because they did not believe in his love and his power to jump in and change things. They mistakenly thought he was distant, far away, and not concerned about their situation. The same loving God today is looking at you and me—at our situations—and is ready to jump in to help us. All we need to do is believe in God's love, to trust in his willingness to help. Ask! Just give him a chance. He is telling us: "I am right here prepared to help you. You need only to ask me." As Jesus told us: "Your Father knows what you need before you ask him " (Matthew 6:8). When we ask, prayer opens us up to his answer.

Prayer

Lord, help me to believe and trust enough to ask. Amen.

Save for the Future

"Blessed are those who trust in the Lord."—JEREMIAH 17:7

....

Most of us plan for the future by investing in a savings account. Jesus also spoke of the importance of storing up treasures—treasures in heaven. That's something we can all do through simple words of trust—prayers of confidence in God's ever-present love. Whenever we trust in his plan for today and tomorrow, we are building up a savings account for those days ahead that may present real challenges and difficult problems. We build up that account by trusting God in small things. Trust him for his love today; trust him for some relatively simple thing—a simple task. Then when life brings troubles that deplete your energy and threaten to leave you feeling emotionally and spiritually bankrupt, your savings account of trust will be more than enough to see you through.

Prayer

Lord, help me to so trust you that I completely abandon myself into your hands. Amen.

Everything Works Out

"We know that all things work together for good for
those who love God"—ROMANS 8:28

One of the most consoling passages found in the New Testament
are the words of St. Paul in his letter to the Romans: "We know
that all things work together for good for those who love God"
(8:28). Because St. Paul experienced his own weakness and sin—
but also God's mercy—he could sympathize with others in their
weaknesses. Notice that St. Paul says *all* things, not some things.
Even our past sins, once we've turned away from them, can be used
by God for the benefit of ourselves or others. Sometimes we can see
that, but often we cannot.

Trust solely in Divine Providence, and all will work out supremely
well. Since God has created our beautiful and endless universe, his
Providence, his loving plans for you and me guide it—and personally guide our daily activities. Trust him, and the more easily his
providential plan will work to your benefit. Trusting his loving
Providence releases his power on my behalf. The greater the trust,
the more the power is at work.

Prayer

Lord, help me see how your Providence always works in my favor.
Amen.

God's Providence

"O taste and see that the Lord is good."—Proverbs 34:8

How do we get over those rough spots in life that we all experience? Are they really part of God's goodness and plan? I learn to see God's providential love working in the very smallest occurrences of my daily life (suddenly finding something I've lost, a kind word from a friend, an unexpected blessing). These small "tastes" of the goodness of the Lord will help me in those moments when adversity strikes and my instinct is to doubt. By seeing God's hand in the small things, I can trust him in those events I don't understand. I believe his word through Isaiah: "For as the heavens are higher than the earth, so are my ways higher than your ways and my thoughts than your thoughts" (Isaiah 55:9).

Prayer

Lord, I pray, help me to see your loving Providence in the smallest things. Amen.

Don't Blame

"And the peace of God, which surpasses all
understanding, will guard your hearts and your
minds in Christ Jesus."—PHILIPPIANS 4:7

It's almost impossible to go through life without being wronged
by someone. If the wrongs people commit penetrate our hearts, it's
usually because they find room there. If suffering makes us bitter
or ill-humored, it's often because our hearts are devoid of faith,
hope, and love. But if our hearts are filled with total trust in God
and love for him and our neighbor, there is little room for evil, hurt,
or harm. Strive for spiritual maturity rooted in prayer and trust in
God's unconditional love. We only waste time blaming the people
and the things around us. Resting in God's love helps us reclaim
peace. The more peace there is in us, the more peace there will be in
our troubled world.

Prayer

Lord, it is difficult at times to maintain your peace in my heart.
Help me to trust in you even more. Amen.

Learn from Others' Faults

"Whoever walks in integrity walks securely."—PROVERBS 10:9

....

Teresa of Avila, the sixteenth-century Spanish saint, was the abbess of a large contemplative community. One of her suggestions for dealing with a difficult person was simply: "Strive yourself to practice with great perfection the virtue opposite the fault that the other has." If someone's lack of patience is bothersome, strive personally to develop within yourself the virtue of patience with others. If you are annoyed by a gossipy person, develop the practice of positive speaking or thoughtful silence. If someone is stingy, begin to develop more charity. The faults of others, if you so choose, can make you a more virtuous person, a better person.

Prayer

Lord, help me not to criticize another's fault but to use it to stimulate the opposite virtue in myself. Amen.

Maintain Your Peace

"And can any of you by worrying add a single hour
to your span of life?"—MATTHEW 6:27

....

We are all familiar with the adage "Haste makes waste." Well, it's true. Yet we always seem to be in a hurry, especially if you are a Type-A personality like I am. And sure enough, we often trip over ourselves. Don't be in such a hurry that you lose your inner peace. It's bad for your physical and mental health. Whatever you're trying to do, it's not as valuable as you and your peace of soul. I try to repeat to myself the counsel of St. Francis de Sales: "Never be in a hurry; do everything quietly and in a calm spirit. Do not lose your inner peace for anything whatsoever, even if your whole world seems upset." For the next few hours, don't lose your inner peace for anything. Begin now. And begin again if you fall away from that peace.

Prayer

Lord, give me the grace to trust in your divine plan in all things. Amen.

Be Reconciled

"My friends, if anyone is detected in a transgression, you who have received the Spirit should restore such a one in a spirit of gentleness. Take care that you yourselves are not tempted."—GALATIANS 6:1

The greatest mistake we humans often make is to become upset and lose our peace. We lose our peace because we want, at any price, to change the people around us. How many married people become agitated and irritated because they would like their spouse not to have this or that fault? The Lord, however, counsels us to bear with patience the faults of others, to try to maintain inner peace. Remember, God himself is working on that person, and God is being very patient. So I must pray for that person, be patient with him or her, and be at peace. And hopefully that person is being patient with me.

Prayer

Holy Spirit, giver of all good gifts, grant me the virtue of charity. Amen.

We Remain in Christ Even after Death

"But the souls of the righteous are in
the hand of God."—WISDOM 3:1

The great Jesuit theologian Karl Rahner wrote:

> The great mistake of many people is to imagine that these
> whom death has taken leave us. They remain! Where are
> they? In the darkness? Oh no! It is we who are in darkness.
> We do not see them, but they see us. Their eyes radiant with
> glory are fixed upon our eyes. Though invisible to us, our
> dead are not absent. They are living near us transfigured into
> light, power and love.

Life beyond this short time on earth is real. We are physical beings
with transcendent, immortal souls. We can find hundreds of studies
of near-death experiences. People who have been clinically dead—
no heartbeat or brain waves for several minutes—come back to life.
They report an experience of their soul journeying to a new, higher
sphere of life; they're totally conscious and peaceful, often encoun-
tering others who have gone before them. When they return, care
for their souls becomes a priority: love for God and for others.

Prayer

Lord, help me to see that this life on earth is not all there is. Give
me the grace necessary to know, love, and serve you in this life so I
may be with you forever in the next. Amen.

Live Your Life without Fear

"Do not let your hearts be troubled, and do not
let them be afraid."—JOHN 14: 27

. . . .

Etty Hillesum was a vibrant young Jewish woman who lived in
Nazi-occupied Amsterdam and died in Auschwitz in 1943. In the
months before she was arrested, she underwent a profound trans-
formation through psychotherapy. She discovered God and refused
to give in to hatred, even when facing the evil of the Holocaust. She
refused to worry about what might be her fate. She journaled: "If
one burdens the future with one's worries, the future cannot grow
organically. I am filled with confidence, not that I shall succeed in
worldly things, but that even when things go badly for me, I shall
still find life good and worth living."

She realized that the fear of suffering causes more pain than the
suffering itself does. About these fears she wrote: "We have to fight
fears daily, like fleas, those many small worries about tomorrow.
for they sap our energy....We must not allow ourselves to become
infested with thousands of petty fears, and worries, so many motions
of no confidence in God. Everything will turn out all right."

Be confident! Trust in God to handle the future.

Prayer

Lord, like Etty, help me to discover you anew so my life can unfold
organically. The future is yours. The present is mine. Help me to live
it well. Amen.

Mistakes Perfect Virtue

"For though they fall seven times, they will rise again; but the wicked are overcome by calamity."—PROVERBS 24:16

Albert Einstein once said, "A person who never made a mistake never tried anything new." Einstein himself failed as a student. Everyone, especially his father, thought he was a failure. As a person who worked with numbers, he figured out that physicists were wrong about light, gravity, and space.

Some of the most faithful people in our society are the men and women who learn from their mistakes and thus grow in virtue. We all make mistakes and plenty of them; so did the saints. We can take the negative path and beat ourselves up or blame someone else. Or we can take the positive path and ask, "What is God teaching me right now?" When our children mess up, don't we ask them, "What did you learn?"

Mistakes are teachable moments coming from an all-loving God. Are you involved in a special project? Keep it up! Don't be afraid of making a mistake. Like Einstein, you'll eventually succeed if you keep trying. Never let your mistakes hold you back!

Prayer

Lord, during my short time in this world, let me see your great love for me in all things: my joys, my successes, my failures, and my mistakes. For I know you love me and want to prepare me well for eternity with you. Amen.

Suffering and Triumph

"I am now rejoicing in my sufferings for your sake, and in my flesh I am completing what is lacking in Christ's afflictions for the sake of his body, that is, the Church."—COLOSSIANS 1:24

....

The Frenchman Pierre de Coubertin founded the modern Olympic Games in 1896. He had these words of guidance for Olympians: "The important thing in life is not the triumph, but the struggle." St. John Paul II said something similar: "We come to truly know ourselves only through adversity and struggle." Some of the most beautiful and peaceful people I've known are those who have struggled for most of their lives with physical disabilities. Through their struggles, they triumphed over the temptations of this world, uniting their struggles with the sufferings of Christ. Struggles are important because through them we perfect the virtues of humility, diligence, and perseverance. All these virtues are necessary if we are to live for eternity with the Church Triumphant in heaven.

Prayer

I thank you, Lord, for the struggles and joys of life. All come from your divine hand and are meant to help me attain the salvation you won for me in your passion and death so that I might be brought into the glory of your Resurrection. Amen.

Trials: God's Loving Discipline

"My child, do not regard lightly the discipline of the Lord, or lose heart when you are punished by him; for the Lord disciplines those whom he loves....He disciplines us for our good, in order that we may share his holiness."—HEBREWS 12:5–6,10

There are times in every life when we find ourselves in situations of trial or difficulty, either affecting us or someone we love. It seems we can do nothing. Perhaps we feel helpless. Yet despite everything, we can continue to believe, hope, and love. Yes, believe that God will not abandon that person; hope in the Lord's faithfulness and power for everything. And we can love by continuing to carry that person in our heart and prayer. We should try to express love in every way available to us. Love is always fruitful. Good fruit will appear sooner or later, in the time of God's plan and God's mercy.

St. Augustine wrote: "Our pilgrimage on earth cannot be exempt from trials." We progress by means of trial. No one knows himself or herself except through difficulties and trials. In those times seek for the opportunity for personal growth. Seek out a trusted friend. Pray for the wisdom to see each trial as a blessing, an opportunity for spiritual growth, from your all-loving Father in heaven.

Prayer

Thank you, loving Father, for the trials of this life. Help me to accept them, grow in virtue and wisdom from them, and always surrender myself to your perfect will. Amen.

The Gift of Humility

"Now there are varieties of gifts, but the same Spirit, and
there are a variety of services, but the same Lord; and there are
varieties of activities, but the same God who activates all
of them in everyone."—1 Corinthians 12:4

One of the easiest mistakes we make in life is to play the Comparison
Game. We can never be happy comparing ourselves to other people.
If, for example, I realize that I am better organized than someone
else, my ego is pumped up. But when I see that someone else has
a better education or job than I do, I'm depressed. My mistake is
that I have not acknowledged my strong points and accepted my
limitations. That's called humility. St. Francis de Sales counseled:
"Be who you are and be that well. Do not wish to be anything but
what you are and try to be that perfectly." You will enjoy inner peace
if you don't play the Comparison Game.

Prayer

Lord, help me to rejoice in the talents and gifts of others and see
that all good gifts are from you and are meant to return to you for
your greater glory and the salvation of souls. Amen.

Humility and Wisdom

"The fear of the Lord is instruction in wisdom, and humility goes before honor."—PROVERBS 15:33

....

The English philosopher Bertrand Russell in the 1930s wrote: "The whole problem with the world is that fools and fanatics are always so certain of themselves, and wiser people so full of doubts." This phenomenon is called the Dunning-Kruger effect, based on studies showing that people with limited knowledge or competence can greatly overestimate their own knowledge or competence, while people with a high degree of competence often underestimate their ability. In spirituality, the antidote to this is the virtue of humility. Humble people have an accurate self-awareness, knowing the truth about the gifts they have and the ones they lack. God's gift of wisdom allows us to cultivate this virtue and bring all our gifts to the world.

Prayer

Lord, you are all-wise, the source of all true wisdom. Help me to grow in the wisdom of self-knowledge. Amen.

I Am Infinitely Valuable

"For it was you who formed my inward parts;
you knit me together in my mother's womb.
I praise you, for I am fearfully and wonderfully made."
—PSALMS 139:13–14

Archbishop Fulton J. Sheen, a leading spiritual teacher—and surprising TV personality—in the 1950s and 1960s, often said that God does not love us because we are valuable. We are valuable because God loves us. Think about that. You and I are valuable whether we think we are or not. The truth is that in the eyes of God, we are more precious than the whole universe put together. I don't have to make myself valuable so God will love me. To recognize how valuable I really am is an act of faith in the reality of God's personal love. We are valuable because God truly loves each of us more than we can imagine.

Prayer

Lord, I thank you for my being and my life. Let me always remember how much you love me by meditating on the price you paid for my salvation. Amen.

God Is All You Need

"My grace is sufficient for you, for power is made
perfect in weakness."—2 CORINTHIANS 12:9

Recently someone who was going through a very difficult time
in her life told me something I hope I never forget. She said,
"Sometimes when your feel like God is all you have, you discover
that God is all you need." She was learning a great lesson. Friends,
finances, and health are wonderful gifts to us from our loving God.
But all will sooner or later pass away. In gratitude we thank God for
his many gifts. By faith he shows us that he has been the giver of
those gifts and that the greatest, most reliable, external, no-fail gift
is himself. We will always have God. Yes, when we feel like all we
have is God, we discover that God is all we need.

Prayer

The Lord is my shepherd; there is nothing I shall want. Amen.

Midlife Crisis

"I will never leave you or forsake you."—HEBREWS 13:5

Sometime during their fifties, many people begin to feel a great inner emptiness. Perhaps it's because they were trying to live by doing, by their accomplishments, while forgetting their true, inalienable identity as children of God, loved not for what they do but for who they are, children, offspring of God. Yes, they are his beloved daughters or sons, whether they do good or cannot yet manage to do much of anything. He loves each of us for ourselves because he has adopted us as his children forever. Our value is not in what we do or in what we have or possess. All that eventually goes away. Our lasting value is in who we are: God's forever beloved son or daughter.

Prayer

Lord, help me to see that the more I can focus on you, the more I begin to understand who I am. Amen.

Pray, Trust, and Don't Worry

"So do not worry about tomorrow, for tomorrow will bring worries of its own. Today's trouble is enough for today."—MATTHEW 6:34

Occasionally someone will share with me their fears—about the economy, the direction of our moral standards, the aftermath of the pandemic. So many things seem out of our control. The apostles of Jesus were in a boat with him and panicked when a huge storm arose at sea threatening to sink them. They awakened Jesus, who immediately calmed the sea and wind and told them, "I am with you—I care—where is your faith and trust in me?" Their fear was gone. God was there and clearly in charge.

The most repeated phrase in the Bible—over two thousand times—is "Fear not." God's messengers can confidently say, "Be not afraid" because they know that God is in charge of history; God is always present and loves us. Jesus said, "Fear is useless, what is needed is trust." And I love the counsel of St. Padre Pio: "Pray, trust, and don't worry!" When we are fearful, we need to trust in God's loving presence and power to help. He cares!

Prayer

Lord, help me to live in this present moment, for it is in the present that you reveal yourself to me. Let me have the wisdom to leave the past to your mercy and the future to your Divine Providence. Amen.

God Is with You

"Let us hold fast to the confession of our hope without wavering, for he who has promised is faithful."—HEBREWS 10:23

Do not be afraid of yourself! Have no fear of all those things that are unique in you. God pitches his tent with you. God is Emmanuel—which means "God is with us." God is with you and your reality, so open yourself to him. And only in the measure you discover your unique gifts will you discover the depths of God's special love for you. There, in the depths of yourself, you will experience that you are not alone. God lovingly and mercifully has entered into the mystery of your humanity—not as a spectator or judge, but as someone who loves you. God is there to heal you, free you, and save you. God will never leave you. God will stay with you, loving you forever.

Prayer

Lord, deepen my faith and trust in your personal presence to me. Amen.

The Best Remedy for Anxiety

"It is the Lord who goes before you. He will be with you; he will not fail you or forsake you. Do not fear or be dismayed."

—DEUTERONOMY 31:8

Most of the time our anxiety stems from a fear of something or someone in the future. The next time it happens to you, try the "Three Ps Remedy":

Prepare—Do what you can now. Simply ponder, *What can I do in a proactive way that makes sense?* Usually one or two things will occur to you. Do them and watch your anxiety begin to shrink.

Present—Live in the present moment, not in the imagined future. Living in the now can help smother the fire of fear.

Pray—Know that God is in of control of the future. God has the power and the love to do what we cannot do. Our Father's love can and does shape the future. Pray and experience the peace that will replace the anxiety, because the God who loves you unconditionally is in control now and in the days ahead.

Prayer

Lord, show me how to prepare, to live in the present moment, and to pray when fear begins to creep in. Amen.

The Poorest

"Happy are those who consider the poor; the Lord delivers them in the day of trouble."—Psalm 41:1

We see poverty everywhere in our world. We notice the poor on our streets. But where is the greatest poverty? For decades Mother Teresa of Calcutta pointed to what she called "the poorest of the poor." She once noted that "loneliness and the feeling of being unwanted is the greatest poverty." That poor person may live next door to you, be in your family, or sit next to you at work. Feed that poor person with your smile or a word of greeting. Take time to visit him or her; call or text that person. You truly can become a blessing because you are lifting that person out of his or her poverty of loneliness or the feeling of being unwanted. You and I can become real blessings to the poor.

Prayer

Lord, help me to recognize those who are emotionally poor and reach out to them. Amen.

Give Generously

"The measure you give will be the measure you get."
—MATTHEW 7:2

....

One of the fundamental laws of human life and of the spiritual life is that the measure we give to others will be the measure we will receive. If I give love and forgiveness, I will receive it, perhaps from others, but most certainly from God. If we refuse to love, or to forgive, we will sooner or later become victims of our own lack of love. The evil we do or wish to others will end up turning against ourselves. God does not punish anyone. People punish themselves. Today, make up your mind to love, to give of yourself to God and to others. Forgive someone. Let your measure to others be bountiful love and sincere forgiveness, and that love and mercy will be poured back to you bountifully.

Prayer

Lord, right now I pray for someone I need to forgive, someone I need to love. Amen.

Let God Take Care of Tomorrow

"You saw how the Lord your God carried you,
just as one carries a child."—DEUTERONOMY 1:31

Be at peace by living in the now. Only when we see the future as a positive reality does it become possible to live well in the present moment. St. Francis de Sales wrote that we should not worry about future events, but look forward to them "with perfect hope in the God to whom you belong. He will protect you. God has protected you thus far. Stay in God's providential hands. And in those situations when you can't walk (so to speak) God will carry you as a loving Father carries a small child."

He taught what Jesus taught: Trust that God is closer to us than we are to ourselves. In Jesus, heaven has reached out to us, and we can reach out to heaven; it is attainable! The reality of heaven means that our life will not end in emptiness. Because I live in the present filled with hope, I am living life well—joyfully, productively, with a smile.

Prayer

Lord, help me to live in the now—the present moment—that's where I'll find you. Thank you for carrying me this far. I believe you will continue to do so. Amen.

Trust God's Providence

"I have inscribed you on the palms of my hands."—Isaiah 49:16

The Lutheran philosopher Søren Kierkegaard had many insightful observations. One was that "life can only be understood backwards, but it must be lived forward." Looking backwards with the eyes of faith, seeing the loving, providential hand of God, I am filled with gratitude in how his unconditional love has guided me through valleys and up mountains. Looking forward, I have great hope and trust that the same God who protected me up to this point will guide my steps tomorrow as well.

Kierkegaard also wrote: "The highest and most beautiful things in life are not to be heard about, nor read about, nor seen but, if one will, are to be lived." Reach out to others in some small way today and become more beautiful yourself, making our world a more beautiful place. All we need to do is remain firmly in the hands of God, the source of all beauty and life.

Prayer

Lord, deepen my faith in your ever-present love for me. Such faith engenders the trust I need to reach out in love to others. Amen.

Growing through Challenges

"When the righteous cry for help, the Lord hears, and rescues them from all their troubles."—PSALM 34:17

No doubt sometimes life is difficult, and we might ask why a loving God would allow these difficulties in our life. It's for the same reason a parent sends his or her five-year-old to school. The parent knows the child may be picked on, lose a friend, or be misunderstood by a teacher. But it's good for the child to have to struggle in order to mature, to develop patience, inner strength, perseverance. The same holds true for us throughout our lives. As St. Augustine wrote, "Without suffering and the challenges in life, we never grow and develop as persons." God holds us by the hand in times of trial. Live in faith and trust in his plans in those difficult situations. Challenges are opportunities for personal growth!

Prayer

Lord, I have grown through my various challenges. Help me to continue to do so. Amen.

Growth through Sacrifice

"It is more blessed to give than to receive."—ACTS 20:35

We grow as persons by giving to others—by loving others—which always requires a free decision to give up something for someone else. Look into history. Abraham Lincoln made many personal sacrifices and faced much criticism because he was determined to make us one nation. In our own experience, isn't it that self-sacrificing mom or dad we most admire? Their decision to sacrifice for their family or others has made them into truly great people who inspire us every day to become more giving and loving people. We grow as persons each time we make even a small self-sacrifice in giving to another, in loving another. And then we begin to experience a most surprising by-product—inner peace.

Prayer

Lord, give me the grace and courage to make those small, personal sacrifices for others. Amen.

Our Restless Hearts

"My soul thirsts for God, for the living God."—Psalm 42:2

Perhaps you have noticed how restless a small child becomes when his or her parents are absent for a while. The child feels that something very precious and much needed is missing: the source of love, embrace, and acceptance that the child began to feel in his or her mother's womb. At the moment of conception, one's soul, one's spiritual self, was also created by the loving hand of God. We instinctively crave that supernatural care, embrace, and love. We are made to love and to be loved by God. The great St. Augustine, after years of searching for that transcendent embrace, wrote: "You have made us for yourself, and our hearts are restless until they rest in you."

Prayer

Lord, show me yourself; help me to find satisfaction in resting in you. Amen.

Trust Anew

"Trust in the Lord forever, for in the Lord God
you have an everlasting rock."—Isaiah 26:4

We were created to love. Whether we are aware of it or not, one
of our deepest aspirations is to give ourselves to another. Yet that
inner drive is often blocked by self-centered, ego-centered selfishness. Caught in that net, we become discouraged—we lose fervor,
zest, and generosity in loving God and neighbor. The remedy is to
rekindle our hope, to rediscover a new trust based on the faith that
God wants to and can do for us (no matter how weak and wretched
we are) more than we can ask for or imagine. "Ask, and it will be
given you" (Matthew 7:7). Feeling discouraged? Then just ask; you
will receive.

Prayer

God, by your own Holy Spirit, rekindle my belief in your readiness
to answer my prayers. Amen.

Time Together

"It is you, my equal , my companion, my familiar friend, with whom I kept pleasant company." —Psalm 55:13–14

A young married man recently told me that he and his wife were going to take a short vacation together without their three children. He told me, "We haven't been alone together since our honeymoon." This is a very wise young couple. All couples need to pay attention and give time to their relationship—without distractions. The stronger their bond, the happier and more secure their children feel. As the old saying goes: "The best way to love your children is to love your spouse." Quality, undistracted time together deepens love, understanding, patience, and commitment. There is no substitute for those precious moments spent deepening an important relationship.

Prayer

Lord, help married couples see how spending quality time together strengthens their bond. Amen.

Parenting by Example

"Train children in the right way,
and when old, they will not stray"—PROVERBS 22:6

It is very important that children learn from their fathers and mothers how to love one another—not in the school, not from the teacher, but from you, the parents. It is very important that you share with your children the joy of your smile. There will be misunderstandings—every family has its crosses, its sufferings—but always be the first to forgive with a smile. Be cheerful! Be happy! In the home, from the parents, especially when the children are small, love is caught, not just taught. Parents, try to grow in patience and love—your children will learn love by catching it.

Prayer

Lord, show parents that their example is the best teacher. Amen.

Availability

"A generous person will be enriched,
and one who gives water will get water."—PROVERBS 11:25

....

A key word in our relationship with other people is *availability*.
Availability is genuine love. Remember how you felt loved, valued,
and appreciated when someone gave you his or her 100 percent
undivided, heartfelt attention? That person chose to be available to
you. A bond was created or strengthened because that person made
the genuine gift to you of his or her own time, or schedule—really,
his or her very self. You were loved. Do the same today. Be available
intentionally to someone who needs your attention and love. Try
to be available with attention and a smile. It will brighten someone
else's day and your own.

Prayer

Lord, you are always available to me. Help me to be available to
others. Amen.

True Friendship

"Some friends play at friendship,
but a true friend sticks closer than one's nearest kin."
—PROVERBS 18:24

One of the greatest gifts we have on this earth is friendship. In fact, Aristotle taught that friendship is *the* greatest gift a person can have. The Book of Proverbs says: "A friend loves at all times, but a brother is born for adversity." Be grateful to God for your good friends, especially the ones who become like brothers or sisters because they were with you and supported you in a time of adversity. In developing new friendships, seek out those with high moral values, even higher than your own. Affirm their values, because others may not appreciate them. That friend needs your friendship as much as you need his or hers.

Prayer

Lord, I thank you for the gift of your friendship. Thank you for my true friends. Amen.

Forgive Quickly

"Be kind to one another, tenderhearted, forgiving one another, as God in Christ has forgiven you."—EPHESIANS 4:32

Friendship is a gift and a challenge. Be grateful that God has placed good friends in your life. Often challenges and differences will arise. Proverbs 17:9 says, "One who forgives an affront fosters friendship, but one who dwells on disputes will alienate a friend." Is there a situation in your life in which a friend has affronted you or the two of you have had a dispute? Be careful! Don't lose a good friend. Forgive the affront. Try to put the dispute behind you. It's a new day! A quarrel between friends, when made up, adds a new tie to friendship.

Prayer

Lord, thank you for being quick to forgive me. Help me to forgive others quickly. Amen.

Part Two

INSPIRATION

Powerful Gifts

"Now faith, hope and love abide, these three; and the
greatest of these is love."—1 CORINTHIANS 13:13

The three Christian virtues of faith, hope, and love bring you and
me into a direct relationship with God. Of course, love is the
greatest of the three, but hope is the most important. If I have faith
in God's intimate personal, presence to me, I have hope. I am free
to love more. And the opposite is true. A world without hope soon
becomes a world without love. Hope is nourished by faith in God's
unconditional love. Faith brings that which seems hopeless within
one's reach. Faith gives birth to hope, which gives birth to love. A
person of faith is not necessarily the one who only believes that
God can do everything, but rather the one who believes that he and
she can obtain everything from God. The saints often taught that
we obtain from God as much as we hope for from him. Hope and
pray with a peace that comes from trusting God's love for you.

Prayer

Please increase in me these powerful gifts from you: faith, hope and
love. I need your help to live them. Amen.

God at the Center

"We know that all things work together for good
for those who love God."—ROMANS 8:28

Instinctively every human being has a hunger for God because each of us has a hunger for happiness. Most of us have discovered that all those things we thought would make us happy might have for a while but faded and kept us searching. St. Augustine wrote of his search: "You have made us for thyself, and our hearts are restless until they rest in thee." Your heart, your life, and mine have a deep capacity for limitless, infinite, pure, irrevocable love. No human being or beings can satisfy that deep yearning. Only God can fill it with his infinite, gentle, unconditional, eternal love. Human interpersonal relationships are great gifts from God. We need the love of others, but we must keep God at the center. We must look to God for that deep peace, happiness, and security that only God can give and not expect it from another limited, imperfect human being. Only God is perfect; humans are not. In daily, peaceful prayer, God continues to fill that capacity. Keep God at the center, and he will put the puzzle of life together for you.

Prayer

Lord, call me often to prayer and reflection so I can keep you at my center. Amen.

Have Hope

"Rejoice in hope, be patient in suffering, persevere in prayer."
—ROMANS 12:12

Why do those people with real, genuine faith seem to be people of peace, people with peace? Because faith in God's unconditional love gives them hope. What is real hope? It's trust that God is right there, close, involved in our lives. One of the saints wrote: "Faith brings what seems hopeless within our reach, then added, "The person of faith is not one who believes that God can do everything, but the one who believes that he or she can obtain everything from God."

The Bible reveals the absolute unconditional and irrevocable love God has for his children. This is shown in Christ who both died and rose again for us. St. Paul wrote: "He loved me, and gave himself for me." Through faith our hearts hold on to that truth and find great trust in God. The more I believe in his love for me, the more I enjoy God's presence. If you believe in God's unconditional, personal love for you, then you believe you can obtain everything from God. That's faith! Faith is the mother of hope, real hope, and from hope peace is born in the human soul.

Prayer

Lord, strengthen my hope in you. Amen.

Hope Brings Life

"For surely I know the plans I have for you, says the Lord,
plans for your welfare and not for harm, to give you
a future with hope."—JEREMIAH 29:11

The brilliant French philosopher Gabriel Marcel wrote: "I almost think that hope is for the soul what breathing is for the living organism. Where hope is lacking, the soul dries up and withers."

Hope is a virtue that is critical for survival in life. We don't last long without it. Without hope we die physically, emotionally, and spiritually. Living involves hope. In his book *Man's Search for Meaning*, Viktor Frankl observed other prisoners in a Nazi concentration camp. He noted that those who had hope in being rescued lived on. Those who gave up died. Be alive! Have hope in something real. And the most real thing is the presence and providential plan of God for you.

Prayer

Lord, help me to grow in belief of your presence and plan for me. Amen.

Love Breeds Hope

"This is my commandment, that you love one another
as I have loved you."—JOHN 15:12

We place some of our hope in other people—family members, friends, co-workers, or neighbors. That feeling of hope and expectation brightens our life. And others are also placing some of their hope, trust, or confidence in you and me. Usually we know, or at least sense, what they hope for from us: a listening ear, compassion, a smile, or something we can actually give them. Our response to fulfill their hope is one word: love. Yes, it is love that moves our mind and heart to answer the hope they place in us. And if we can't totally fulfill their hope, our love itself will fill the gaps. Love and pray for those who place some hope in you. They won't be disappointed because they will sense your love for them.

Prayer

Lord, inspire me to love so that you can inspire the hope others need. Amen.

Rejoice in Hope

"Happy are they who make the Lord their trust." —PSALM 40:4

Hope is essential for survival. I knew a Catholic nun who was physically challenged. She told me that she had applied to seventeen religious orders, and the eighteenth accepted her application. She persevered. She had hope based on the call she felt from God. She survived the refusals. She had hope because she prayed to our loving Father in heaven. Prayer strengthens hope in God's hand when all else seems hopeless. She lived Psalm 71: "For you, O Lord, are my hope, my trust, O Lord, from my youth. Upon you have I leaned from my birth." Like that nun, we should persevere in prayer to our loving heavenly Father to reinforce our hope for the future. It's all in his loving hands.

In the Hebrew Scriptures the Jewish people were called the "People of Hope." Pick up the Jewish book of prayer, the Psalms, and meditate on the messages of hope found there. For example, "But I have calmed and quieted my soul, like a weaned child with its mother; my soul is like the weaned child that is with me. O Israel, hope in the Lord from this time on and forevermore" (Psalm 131:2–3). With prayer comes hope. With hope comes life!

Prayer

Father, help me to truly abandon with the greatest trust every moment of my life into your loving hands. Amen.

The Anchor of Hope

"Now faith is the assurance of things hoped for, the conviction of things not seen." —HEBREWS 11:1

The writer of the Book of Psalms sums up his reason for hope in Psalm 56:9–11: "This I know, that God is for me. In God, whose word I praise, … in God I trust; I am not afraid." There you have it. The person who believes and trusts in God, in my observation, has far less fear because he or she senses God's presence, care, and protection. In the Scriptures, hope is visualized as an anchor. By hope we are anchored to Christ, so we don't go adrift. He comes to us spiritually to be our anchor amid the storms of life. Be open to him.

Prayer

Lord, it is so easy for me to drift. Be my anchor. Amen.

Love's Challenge

"This is my commandment, that you love one another as I have loved you. No one has greater love than this, to lay down one's life for one's friends."—JOHN 15:12–13

....

The word *love* is used a lot. We hear it every day. Love your neighbor, love your country, and for Christians, love even your enemies. We all need to be loved; we all need to love because others also need to be loved. But what is love? Love is a choice, a decision to go out of oneself and look at what would be best for someone else instead of what appears to be best for me. That's true love, and we all know that. Don't worry about those positive feelings; they will soon be there in a deeper and long-lasting way.

St. John Paul II had an interesting description of love: "Love is a challenge God throws to us." But why would loving my spouse, or child, or friend, or a stranger be a challenge? Because love, as John Paul defined it, is the sincere gift of oneself to another. I must forget myself or my schedule, my needs, or my comfort in favor of someone else. That's the challenge God throws at us. Ultimately, by loving others in this way, we are showing God how much we love him. Choose to go outside yourself today for another person. You and they will be better and happier for it!

Prayer

Lord, I need your Holy Spirit so I can love as you love. Help me to choose the best for others. Amen.

Happiness

"You show me the path of life. In your presence
there is fullness of joy."—Psalm 16:11

Eleanor Roosevelt once said something that is very true: "Happiness
is not something that we can directly acquire. It's a by-product of
something else. It seeps into our consciousness and emotions when
we choose to do that right thing, the best thing." We basically
become happy when we do our best as parents or at work, or when
we reach out to help someone, or fulfill our responsibilities, whether
others notice it or not. Then suddenly, strangely, we are happy. Don't
go after happiness directly. It will elude you. Just try to be the best
version of yourself. Do everything with peace and for the right
reason and happiness will be there as a by-product.

Prayer

Lord, teach me to live with love and happiness will follow. Amen.

Gentle Strength

"Blessed are the meek, for they will
inherit the earth."—MATTHEW 5:5

....

"Nothing is stronger than gentleness, and nothing is more gentle than real strength." This saying came from the experience of the great saint of gentleness, Francis de Sales, who lived in the early seventeenth century. Nothing is stronger than gentleness. Think of how you can be strong in a situation or with another person. Then try to be gentle! Remember, the stronger person is the one who is gentler. True gentleness is a sign of true strength. Nothing is stronger than gentleness, and nothing is more gentle than real strength—think about that often today! Try it!

Prayer
Lord, your gentleness always won. Help me to be gentle. Amen.

A Smile Is the First Step to Love

"A glad heart makes a cheerful countenance." —PROVERBS 15:13

Our world today seems to be a war zone. It seems as though peace has gone out the window. But we can bring it back. St. Teresa of Calcutta walked into contentious situations in various countries. She carried with her the first step to peace. It's simple, and we can all do it. She said, "Peace begins with a smile." That means peace begins with me and within me, and I want to share it with you. Most of the time I can be a joyful person. I can have that joy because I have hope. Occasionally I will feel some kind of "affliction." But I am patient. It will pass. I can always have that small smile on my face, almost visible only to myself.

The smile, Mother Teresa often said, is truly the first step in love. When someone smiles and says hello to me, down deep it seems to draw me out of myself. I feel noticed, valued, communicated with, acknowledged. Our world needs love and so do your family and friends. They need and want your love. Your smile must not only be the first step in love, but it could also be the next step as well. Take that next step for your family and friends. Take the first step with your smile. Share it with the next person you meet. They may need the love that's behind that smile.

Prayer

Lord, help me to always carry some joy in my heart and let it grow into a small smile. Amen.

Live Lighthearted

"This is the day the Lord has made. Let us rejoice
and be glad in it." —PSALM 118:24

C.S. Lewis, one of the great Christian scholars and writers of the twentieth century, wrote that the goal of the Christian is simple: to proclaim the reality of God's kingdom of love and joy. He said that the power of choice makes evil possible. But choice is also the only thing that makes possible any love, goodness, or joy worth having. How can I become a joyful person, a more lighthearted person, even cheerful? Such an attitude adds to my own mental and physical health and helps to create a fresh and positive environment around me.

Another English scholar and saint, John Henry Newman, taught that the graces of joy are gifts from God, but we can invite such gifts by being a person of gratitude. The more thankful I am for the greatest or smallest gifts I have, the more joy will seep into my life, my personality. Become joyful by being grateful. Newman's teaching was strong—he said not only is it good to be joyful, but it is wrong to be otherwise. He told everyone that cheerfulness and lightness of heart are not only privileges but our duty whatever our situation. Let's work on being cheerful and joyful. It changes everything!

Prayer

Lord, teach me that I can live with a light heart because your love is in control. Amen.

The Importance of Small Things

"It [the mustard seed] is the smallest of all the seeds, but when it has grown it is the greatest of shrubs…"—MATTHEW 13:32

St. Francis de Sales wrote, "Even little actions are great when they are done well." Anything we do for the right reason makes those small tasks great. Try always to have love for others, family, business, and a healthy love for oneself. Don't sell short those small tasks that fill most of your days. Create a habit of looking for those simple things around the house, at work, or in the neighborhood that can be done simply, quietly, and with the power of great love. Don't pass up the opportunities that are always there! Start with that small task in front of you now.

Prayer

Lord, help me to see the value in small tasks. Amen.

Do a Small Act of Love

"Let all that you do be done in love."—1 CORINTHIANS 16:14

God sees every act of love as great. Today do a small act of love for someone. Open a door for someone, or just say "please" or "thank you." Believe that however small it seems, it is great in the eyes of God. Most of us are not called to do great deeds, but we can all do small things done with great love. Few of us are in a position to help hundreds of others—here or abroad—but we can reach out and help that one friend or neighbor or relative or stranger or child. As Mother Teresa often said, "If you cannot feed a hundred people, then just feed one."

Prayer

Lord, help me to see the greatness in your eyes of my small acts of love and kindness. Amen.

Each Drop Adds to the Ocean

"Come, you that are blessed by my Father, inherit the kingdom prepared for you from the foundation of the world; for I was hungry and you gave me food..."—Matthew 25:34–35

There is so much need for good today that it can be overwhelming. We think, *What good is my small part?* Do not sell yourself short on your effort, small as it may seem. That smile you gave your new neighbor may seem small to you, but it might have meant a whole lot to that neighbor. Maybe that kind word or smile released a flood of self-confidence, joy, peace, and affirmation that your neighbor needed at that moment. It may seem like just a drop in the ocean, but every ocean is fed with small streams.

Mother Teresa, from her own experience, told others: "Be faithful in small things because it is in them that your strength lies." She had the eyes of faith to see the immeasurable dignity and value of each person. She could see the glory of God shining through people discarded by society. Her faith made each person the most important person in the world at that moment. Small thing? Look at the strength of character she developed over the years. What is that "small thing" in your life that God is calling you to be faithful to?

Prayer

Lord, help me to always remember that all I have comes from you, and when I give to others, I am really giving back to you. Amen.

Where Do We Find God?

"The heavens are telling the glory of God, and the firmament proclaims his handiwork."—PSALM 19:1

Our modern culture is often cut off from nature. We live in a world that is reduced to a universe of concrete, tarmacs, steel, and screens. Sometimes we feel like a prisoner in a virtual or fabricated world instead of being in contact with nature, with God's creation. We are in danger of being cut off from God himself. It's amazing how many saints have heard the voice of God gently speak to them through the beauty of God's creation.

St. Francis of Assisi saw the presence of God in all of creation. The great mystic St. Teresa of Avila said that she always had two books when she went to pray: the Bible and nature. On those days when the Scriptures seemed to offer no new inspiration, she would turn to nature. Just as the Scripture would tell her of God's strength in his creation and the gentleness of Jesus in speaking to children, so she would see his majesty in a snowcapped mountain and his beauty in a rose or a tulip. Nature is often called "the footprint of God." Look at nature, and you will discover something about the Creator.

Prayer

Lord, open my eyes to see your footprint in the beauty of creation. Help me today to appreciate you through the world you have created. Amen.

Greater Things

"Very truly, I tell you, the one who believes in me will
also do the works that I do."—JOHN 14:12

I know a wonderful, brilliant Catholic nun who wrote about
moving from self-reliance to prayer. She wrote, "How could they
abase themselves in this way? Standing tall and being captain
of one's own soul was a sort of cultural absolute. Later I was to
realize how really dignified it is for a person to pray—how much
greater stature we have because a perfect God takes our words so
seriously." Too much self-reliance or activity without prayer leads to
fatigue and discouragement. Move from the unbalance of total self-
reliance to the balance of prayer and trust in God's care and presence.
This nun understood the statement of the great St. Augustine: "I
was born for greater things."

Prayer

Lord, help me to move from mediocrity to greater things. Amen.

Become Your Saint

"Since we are surrounded by so great a cloud of witnesses, ...
let us run with perseverance the race that is set before us."
—HEBREWS 12:1

The saints have so much wisdom to share with us about human nature and the greatness to which each of us is called. Pope Francis put it this way: "We are not alone. The Church is made up of countless brothers and sisters who have gone before us who, through the action of the Holy Spirit, are involved in the affairs of those who still live down here." They are very close and involved in our lives.

We often complain about the emptiness and tedium of daily life. Yet the saints teach us to see in this feeling a sign that God has made us for something more than this world can give. People often say, "I'm no saint." But what does it mean to be a saint? Bathing and caring for lepers and the dying as Mother Teresa did? Leading liberation movements? Praying all day in a monastery? Pope Francis says, "No! Simply do your duties well each day, pray, go to work, take care of your children, keep your heart open to God in your suffering and struggles. This is how we become saints." We must do everything with a heart open to God's will, so that even in sickness and suffering, even amidst struggles, we do it all for love of God.

Prayer

Lord, make me the saint you plan me to be. Amen.

A Heart at Peace

"Do not worry about anything, but in everything by prayer and
supplication with thanksgiving let your requests be made
known to God. And the peace of God, which surpasses all
understanding, will guard your hearts and your
minds in Christ Jesus."—PHILIPPIANS 4:6–7

I think that sometimes good people are too hard on themselves.
Their real fault is that they let their inner peace slip away. Big
mistake! Without God's peace we begin to allow demonic thoughts
of how bad we are beat us up. The solution comes from this advice
from St. Francis de Sales: "Keep your heart open and always in
the hands of Divine Providence, whether for great things or small,
obtain for your heart more and more the spirit of gentleness and
tranquility. The more we abandon ourselves trustingly into his providence will his providence work for us."

Prayer

Lord, you are the master of peace. You hold my life in your hands,
and your love for me is infinite. Let me never doubt your ways and
trust always in your Divine Providence. Amen.

Be an Instrument of Peace

"Peace I leave with you; my peace I give to you. I do not give to you as the world gives. Do not let your hearts be troubled, and do not let them be afraid."—JOHN 14:27

When society is disrupted, we all feel somewhat off balance, fearful, or insecure. The best thing is not to crawl into ourselves. We all have something to contribute. A powerful gift can come from your heart: peace. Only the person who has interior peace can really help his or her neighbor. Your thoughts and actions of love will build up the people around you. How can there be love and peace in my family, neighborhood, or workplace if is not first in my own heart? You and I will build up those around us today if we pray to God for his love and peace to fill our minds and hearts.

St. Francis of Assisi encouraged warring factions to pray, "Lord, make me an instrument of your peace." Pray that prayer now and often. And watch how God answers that prayer for you. Watch how in some way you will become an ambassador of peace.

Prayer

Lord, I know that the world can never know peace without you, our Prince of Peace. Let me always be your instrument of peace. Amen.

Light Your Candle

"Let your light shine before others."—MATTHEW 5:16

Back in the 1950s, an Irish priest, Fr. Patrick Peyton, gathered large crowds in stadiums across the country in the evening for prayer together. As it grew dark, he would light a small candle in the middle of the field. His message spoke for itself: It's better to light one small candle than to curse the darkness. We can see darkness all around us, but don't waste time cursing in despair! That's useless. Light a small candle—a positive word or thought or that three-word prayer, "Lord, help us."

A candle loses none of its own light when it lights another candle. It's a great description of what happens to us when we extend ourselves to one another. Yes, we are at times fearful that we will lose something of ourselves when we give ourselves—our time, our attention, our talent, or our treasure to someone else. But we lose nothing. We are, in fact, more our true selves. We are growing in our own souls. . . . That deep inner peace and joy within us is the light we never lose when we love and extend ourselves to another person. Not to worry; nothing lost. Both you and the other person gain. So, intentionally light someone's candle by an act of selfless love today. Become your beautiful self.

Prayer

Lord, help me to do something positive, to be a light and not curse the darkness. Amen.

Your Light Drives Out Darkness

"Hatred stirs up strife, but love covers all offenses."
—PROVERBS 10:12

Our country has been blessed with great leaders who, in their day, effected change through peaceful means. One such leader was Dr. Martin Luther King Jr. He led the civil rights movement that affirmed the dignity of African Americans under the law and did away with unjust laws. Dr. King shared his wisdom with us and truly lived it. He once wisely taught that "returning violence for violence multiplies violence, adding deeper darkness to a night already devoid of stars. Darkness cannot drive out darkness. Only light can do that."

Unfortunately, we see hatred being fomented between classes of people, hatred based on the color of one's skin—or one's political preferences, or one's religious beliefs. We should follow Dr. King's advice. Hatred puts gasoline on the fire of hatred. Love is the water that drowns it out. Love is a choice. Choose to drown out hatred whenever or wherever it appears. Choose to love. Hatred and love cannot coexist. Be that much needed light in your community today.

Prayer

Grant me, Lord, the humility to allow your light to shine through my life. I need more of your love to drown out the hatred I encounter. Amen.

Where Is Your Treasure?

"Where your treasure is, there will your heart be also."
—MATTHEW 6:21

The Jewish *Shema* prayer is quoted by Jesus as the number-one commandment and first principle in fulfilling our reason for existing: Love God alone above all things, above everyone and everything. Put God first, and all else will fall into place. God's personal love for you and me cannot stop or be shut off. Like the sun, it's always beaming down on us. When I open up and choose a loving relationship with God, his love penetrates my heart, directs my mind to truth, and guides my every step securely.

A renowned Jesuit priest, Pedro Arrupe, once wrote: "Nothing is more practical than finding God, that is, falling in love with God in a quite final and absolute way. . . . What you are in love with, what seizes your imagination, will affect everything. It will decide what you will get out of bed for, what you do with your evenings, how you will spend your weekend, what you read, whom you know, what breaks your heart, and what amazes you with joy and gratitude."
Fall in love and stay in love with God, and it will decide everything. Love God with all your heart, mind, and soul—a very smart decision.

Prayer

Help me, Lord, to love you with all my mind, all my soul, and all my strength. Amen.

Spread Love

"Little children, let us love, not in word or speech,
but in truth and action."—1 JOHN 3:18

St. Teresa of Calcutta's passion was to love, help, and care for the "poorest of the poor," as she called them. She began by going into the slums of Calcutta and helping the lepers, the poor, the sick, and the dying. This tiny woman, less than five feet tall, had only prayer and love as the tools for her calling. She once said, "Spread love wherever you go. Let no one ever come to you without leaving happier."

You and I can spread love by taking two simple steps: Step one is prayer, and step two is focus. Before you meet someone or are in contact with him or her, first pray for God's love to shine through you. Then try to focus on that person's situation, needs, and thoughts. They will sense your genuine concern and love for them.

How to start? First, smile when you meet him or her; second, truly listen; and third, speak the truth with gentleness. That's the way to create a friendship and bring others into the joy we have in our relationship with God. The result? No one will ever come to you without leaving happier.

Prayer

Lord, help me to spread love today—your love in me and through me. Help me to truly love everyone I meet. Amen.

Live with Love

"Truly I tell you, just as you did it to one of the least of these, ... you did it to me."—MATTHEW 25:40

Mother Teresa of Calcutta was awarded the Nobel Peace Prize in 1979 and given the Medal of Freedom by President Reagan in 1985. She was canonized a saint in 2016. She spent her life loving the poorest of the poor. She never criticized people, governments, or individuals for faults that might have contributed to sickness or poverty. She once said: "If you judge people, you have no time to love them."

If I feel like criticizing someone, that person probably needs my help, my love, and maybe my prayer. Love helps; judging negatively doesn't. Prayer helps—and prayer works! Instead of judging someone, take the time to love that person. That attitude of love will help that person— and help you as well.

Prayer

Lord, open my eyes to see you in the very least of those I encounter. Give me the wisdom to love others instead of judging them. Amen.

Be the First to Love

"Let each of you look not to your own interests, but to
the interests of others."—PHILIPPIANS 2:4

....

When I teach children, I often hold up my hand and say five words:
"Be the first to love." On the playground, at home, or in school—be
the first to love! Now you are inviting Jesus into the situation. For
adults, too, be the first to love: at home, or at work, at the mall, or
in the car—especially when things get difficult or tense. Be the first
to love—to listen, to forgive, to see the good in another. Bring Jesus
into the situation. Be the first to love. Your love diffuses difficult
situations and opens the door to peace. Be the first to love!

Prayer

Lord, help me more and more to be the first to love. Amen.

Quiet Reflection

"Whenever you pray, go into your room and shut the door and pray to your Father who is in secret, and your Father who sees in secret will repay you."—MATTHEW 6:6

Many people give their minds and hearts a dose of refreshment each day by treating themselves to a few quiet, meditative moments of devotion or prayer, usually at about the same time and place each day. The effects are amazing! Family cares seem to become less stressful, love between spouses becomes more sincere, love for our country and its people is more devoted, and even our daily work seems to be more pleasant and agreeable. A daily dose of prayer and devotion works silent wonders in our lives. If you don't yet do it, try it for a week. Experience the difference it makes. If it works for a week, it will probably grow and have an increasing influence for the weeks and months ahead. Try it! Experience the positive results.

Prayer

Lord, let me see the wisdom of prayerful silence. Amen.

How Do We Find God?

"Listen and hear my voice; pay attention, and
hear my speech."—ISAIAH 28:23

....

We often are deaf to God's presence, loving inspirations, guidance, tenderness, and mercy because of the noise around us and inside us. Create your own space for silence where you can be alone and quiet today. Let God find you there in the silence. Shut out the external noise, as well as the noise inside you, and listen carefully. God's voice is like a gentle, peaceful breeze. Be silent, for silence is the language of God. We think of prayer as speaking to God, but if it's real communication, then we have to give God a chance to speak, to inspire, to heal, to guide, to forgive, and to help us. Mother Teresa wrote: "We need to find God, and he cannot be found in noise and restlessness. God is a friend of silence. See how mature the trees, the flowers, and the grass have grown in silence. See the stars, the moon, and the sun—how they move in silence. We need silence." Take some quiet time, and in that silence find God—or let God find you.

Prayer

Lord, help me to encounter you in the language of silence. Amen.

Prayer: A Loving Conversation

"Draw near to God, and he will draw near to you."—JAMES 4:8

Over the years people have asked me, "What is prayer?" I like to quote St. Teresa of Avila, who described prayer as "a loving conversation with the one who I know loves me." It's a love-talk with God. With the eyes of faith, I see his acts of love in my life. Love draws love. I spontaneously want to love him in return. When I pray, first I thank God for his love and spend time simply saying, "I love you too." Secondly, I try to listen for God's words, inspirations, and ideas, usually by prayerfully reading the Scriptures. And finally, I ask for God's support and guidance. Try praying like this: Thank, listen, and ask. It's a great prayer formula.

Another way to pray is with the acronym ACTS: Adoration, Contrition (for our sins), Thanksgiving, and Supplication (asking for what we or others need). On different days we might pray with more emphasis on one or two of these than on the others. Let your heart and God's love lead to the prayer you need.

Prayer

Lord, show me how to draw near to you. Amen.

Pray with Your Body

"Do you not know that your body is a temple of
the Holy Spirit?"—1 CORINTHIANS 6:19

Have you ever thought of praying with your body? We often reserve prayer for our minds or souls, which is where our conversations with God begin. But we are not pure spirits, as are the angels. We also have bodies, and therefore we can pray with our bodies. For example, simply folding our hands is a prayer, kneeling is a prayer, and opening our arms to heaven is a prayer. Prostrating our bodies facedown before God is a prayer; Jesus often prayed that way. All these express our desire to connect with our loving God. They often strengthen our mental prayer. Today offer at least one body prayer as an expression of the love of God in your heart. Fold your hands in prayer or kneel for a minute. Your body is praying—you are praying.

A very helpful prayer at night, even while lying in bed, is the Sign of the Cross. As I touch my forehead, I say, "Father, thank you for your blessings of today." As I touch my heart, I say, "Son Jesus, forgive my sins and shortcomings," and as I touch my shoulders, I pray, "Holy Spirit, inspire and guide me tomorrow." It's a perfect way to put ourselves into the arms of our loving God as we drift off to sleep under his watchful gaze. Try this simple prayer tonight. It is a beautiful way to have a peaceful night's sleep.

Prayer

Lord, show me how to use my body in prayer to you. Amen.

Prayer Opens Me Up

"You shall be like a watered garden."—Isaiah 58:11

Sometimes in our spiritual life, our internal life, our hearts feel cramped. Very often we need to seek no other reason than the fact that we are refusing to go outside ourselves to love, and especially to forgive generously. Our resentments imprison us in a net that will strangle us. To get free, we must pray for the generosity to love and forgive. God's help will set us free to be filled with limitless oceans of his love and life. Through Isaiah, God promises, "You shall be like a watered garden, like a spring of water, whose waters never fail." Imprisoned in an internal net? Ask for the grace to humbly pray and forgive.

Prayer

Lord, fill me to the brim with your Holy Spirit's gifts of prayer and mercy. Amen.

Prayer Made Simple

"I pray that the God of our Lord Jesus Christ, the Father of glory,
may give you a spirit of wisdom and revelation as you
come to know him."—EPHESIANS 1:17

Many people have a Bible but do not know how to use it for personal prayer. Here's a very simple formula that may help you. First, find a place where you can be alone—perhaps a room in your house or a special corner. Second, pick a passage from the Scriptures, maybe one of the psalms, a chapter from one of the Gospels, a letter of St. Paul, or something from the Old Testament. If you don't know where to begin, look at the readings assigned to Mass for that day.

Finally, ask for whatever is on your heart. God is listening! Then think, *What is the Lord saying to me or about me? About this situation?* Start with ten minutes a day in the same place. You'll begin developing the habit of prayer. Stay with it. Watch how peaceful you become as you are drawn closer to God and to yourself.

Prayer

Lord, give me the grace to pray. Help me. Amen.

Be Attentive to God

"Seek the Lord and his strength, seek his presence continually."—1 CHRONICLES 16:11

Prayer can be defined with one word: *attention*. If your attention is on God the Father or Jesus or the angels and saints, you are praying, even if it's only for five seconds. It's a prayer because you are raising your mind and heart to God. Your attention is on God. You can say a quick word or two, such as "Thank you, Lord," "Help me Lord," "I know you are here," or "I know you are in charge." If you have turned your attention to God, you are praying.

If you need some structure to your prayer, try these three steps. First, realize that God is present. He's not up in the sky somewhere. God is with you, within you, present to you. Second, realize he loves you. He wants to communicate his unconditional love to you. He wants to hug you, to hold you. Third, believe that God is interested in your day and wants to guide you. He is present, he loves you, and he is guiding you.

Prayer

Help me to pray simply, knowing that you are closer to me than I am to myself. Amen.

Morning Prayer

"Listen to the sound of my cry, my King and my God,
for to you I pray."—PSALM 5:2

....

There is a wonderful passage in the Bible that can set you out on the right foot each day: "O Lord, in the morning you hear my voice; in the morning I plead my case to you, and watch" (Psalm 5:3). There are the three simple truths in this passage to remember in the first few minutes after you wake up. First, our loving Father is listening; he's waiting to hear from you. Second, place your requests before God. He's waiting for you to ask so you can be open to his answers. Third, walk through the day "watching in expectation" because God is already answering—sometimes even before we ask. He will answer—in his way and in his timing. As St. Augustine wrote: "God will give me either what I ask or something better because God is my loving Father."

Prayer

Lord, help me to trust your timing in answer to my prayers. Amen.

The Prayer of Jesus

"Lord, teach us to pray."—LUKE 11:1

The disciples of Jesus asked him to teach them how to pray. He taught them what we call the Lord's Prayer. That prayer is the perfect prayer. It contains everything a prayer should have. Pray it devoutly and think about what you are praying. For example, the first words are directed not to an indifferent Higher Power that may or may not be listening to you or me. No, God is a loving, caring, providential, powerful, gentle Father. St. Paul, like Jesus, calls him "Abba" or "Papa"—the intimate speech of a small child to a loving dad. We pray, "Thy will be done." And we believe his will is expressed in all his loving actions, his Providence. God's will for us is to be his true children, to resemble our Papa, to be loving as he is. When we pray the Lord's Prayer, we ask for God's strong, gentle arms to surround us and our Father's strong hand to guide us. The perfect prayer!

Prayer

Our Father in heaven, holy is your name. Help me to be a good child of yours. Amen.

Living in God

"Ever since the creation of the world his eternal power and divine nature, invisible though they are, have been understood and seen through the things he has made."—Romans 1:20

....

The greatest ancient Greek philosophers, Aristotle and Plato, taught that a powerful and intelligent Being was the First Cause of everything and was Pure Goodness. St. Paul spoke to the Greeks of his time about their Unknown God, in whom "we live and move and have our being" (Acts 17:28). Even in our world today, many scientists believe in an absolute, powerful, intelligent Being that began the universe and keeps it going. Most cosmologists agree that a brilliant, powerful Supreme Being began our universe some 13.8 billion years ago in what's called the "Big Bang."

God is the One who gives power and being to all that exists. And were it not for his sustaining presence, all things would cease to exist. Today, consider this reality: You are in God, surrounded and encompassed by God, yes, swimming in God. You are swimming in the love that sustains you and me moment by moment.

Prayer

Thank you, Lord, for my life—life within your life! Amen.

Ever-Present Unconditional Love

"The Lord, the Lord, a God merciful and gracious,
slow to anger, and abounding in steadfast
love and faithfulness."—EXODUS 34:6

....

While there is widespread belief in some Higher Power controlling all of existence, as Christians we believe that Jesus has revealed some key characteristics of God. Some of these he drew from his own Jewish tradition. First, God is unconditional love; he puts no conditions or requirements on his love for us. Second, God's mercy triumphs over his judgment. And third, God does not punish us for our sins; he doesn't "get even." The consequences of our sins can feel like punishment, but this is not God's will for us. God is a merciful Father, a Son who touches us with that mercy, and a Holy Spirit who is Unconditional Love. These aspects of God's nature reveal to us the greatness and beauty of God.

Prayer

Lord, thank you for showing me time and time again that you are real, that you are here, that you care for me. Amen.

The Gifts of Reason and Revelation

"So God created humankind in his image, in the image
of God he created them."—GENESIS 1:27

God communicates with you and me all the time. He does so through two gifts—the two Rs—Reason and Revelation. Reason, our ordinary and careful reasoning, figuring things out, is God's way of directing us. When good reasoning tells me to do this, or say that, or avoid something or someone, or simply speak the truth, God is lovingly giving me guidance. Reason also asks why: Why do I exist? Where am I going? What is my ultimate destiny? How do I get there? God gives us the answer to these questions through revelation. I exist to grow in God's love; my destiny is eternal joy in the community of heaven; I get there with God's help on life's journey. God has personally come to us in the humanity of his Son, Jesus Christ. He came to touch us with his unconditional love and can take us by the hand to guide our steps on life's journey—to forgive, affirm, and inspire. Reason and revelation go together. God's words to us make sense; studying God's words help us to think clearly about things.

Prayer

Lord, thank you for the gift of reason. Help me to use it well. Thank you for your revelation that makes life understandable. Amen.

What Is Truth?

"For this I was born, and for this I came into the world;
to testify to the truth. Everyone who belongs to
the truth listens to my voice."—JOHN 18:37

St. John Paul II visited our country several times and left us with some words of wisdom. As a student he earned degrees in both theology and philosophy. He studied the concept of truth. What is the truth? Truth is the conforming of one's mind to what something really is, not what one wants it to be. God is truth itself. Jesus said: "I am the way, and the truth, and the life" (John 14:6). Since Jesus Christ is the truth, St. John Paul taught that truth has its own force. So, think and speak the truth. It has its own force, and truth will ultimately come to the surface, shining forth like a candle in a dark room. Remember, truth isn't just a concept; it has a name: Jesus.

Prayer

Lord Jesus, I want to hear your voice. Help me conform my mind and heart to you that I may know and boldly speak only truth. Amen.

What Is Faith?

"Now faith is the assurance of things hoped for, the conviction of things not seen."—HEBREWS 11:1

....

You and I know people of faith. But what is faith? Faith is accepting as true what another says. I believe that George Washington was our first president. I never saw or met him, but I believe historians; I have faith in the testimony of those who knew him. Christian faith is similar; I believe in the words and testimony of those who knew and saw Jesus and passed on his teachings accurately. By faith, I say yes to the teachings of Jesus, as I have received them, and I choose to believe in him personally as risen from the dead. In this way, faith in his teachings calls my heart to believe and love. Faith then moves from the head into the heart. That is the essence of faith.

Prayer

Lord, help my reason to accept what is true. Help my heart to choose him in whom I believe. Amen.

Religious Beliefs

"Whoever is not against us is for us."—MARK 9:40

· ·

It is important that each of us respects the religion of our neighbor. St. Teresa of Calcutta wrote: "There is only one God, and he is God to all….Some in our country call God Ishwar or Allah. Each one of us has to recognize that God created us for greater things, such as to love and to be loved; regardless of our religion, if we are open to love and to be loved, then life has depth and meaning." That happens when we sincerely strive to live our religious beliefs and respect those of others. What are your religious beliefs? If you have none, then go and peacefully search for them, asking the Lord to guide you.

Prayer

Lord, help me to live my beliefs and to respect those of other religions. Amen.

The Wonder in Science

"He himself is before all things, and in him all
things hold together."—COLOSSIANS 1:17

When I was a seminarian, one of my classmates was a nuclear
chemist from Iowa State University. He decided to become a
priest when he discovered the intricate details and the beauty of
chemical reactions, particularly nuclear reactions. He saw the great
power and absolute Reason beyond us that makes all this happen.
Scientific discoveries are a wonderful gift to all of us. They show
forth the wisdom of the Creator. Albert Einstein discovered this
when he observed: "In the laws of nature, there is revealed such
a superior person that everything that has arisen out of human
thought and arrangement [planning] is the emptiest reflection in
comparison to it."

Thank God for the progress of science and the insights of religion.
They are complementary and reinforce each other. Science answers
the question "What?" Religion answers the questions "Who?" and
"Why?" Science gives us knowledge, which is power. Religion gives
us wisdom, which is control. Science deals with observable data;
religion deals with values. Science and religion complement one
another, and we need both!

Prayer

Lord, thank you for the work of scientists. They uncover for us the
wonders of your creating hand. Amen.

Part Three

MOTIVATION

Become Your True Self

"Your word is a lamp to my feet and a light to my path."
—PSALM 119:105

Let's face it! We are all a bit of a mystery to ourselves. In the fifth century BC, Greek philosophers had an inscription on the doorposts of their schools that read: "Know Thyself." Christianity took it a step further and said that the key to knowing oneself is love, the sincere gift of oneself to another.

To know the deepest, most truthful realities about myself, I must come to know and be loved by my loving Creator. In Jesus, God took on a human nature to relate to me. Knowing that God loves me personally helps me to know who I really am. I am God's own child destined to grow in love for him and others in this life and to spend my joyous destiny with him and others in heaven.

Prayer

Lord, help me to know myself as you know me. Amen.

Look in the Mirror

"[Do not] think of yourself more highly than you ought to think,
but to think with sober judgment."—ROMANS 12:3

We grow each day in giving and receiving love from others and from the God who loves us. Each time I make a choice to venture outside myself and think the best and do the best for someone else, I see and experience the beautiful person I really am inside! The mystery of myself begins to unfold whenever I choose to love.

Sometimes I need a mirror to help me see who I really am in any given moment. A friend of mine in his mid-nineties has one answer: "Your best mirror is your best friend's eyes." Others can help us to know ourselves, especially our best friends. We trust them, and we know that when they speak the truth to us, it only strengthens the honesty between us. It often tells us who we are.

Prayer

Lord, help me to see the person of beauty I am becoming as I choose to love others. Give me a good friend who can be a true mirror for me. Amen.

Good to Great

"For surely I know the plans I have for you, says the Lord, plans
for your welfare and not for harm."—JEREMIAH 29:11

....

We only go through life once, and we want to make the most of it,
the very best of it. The key is recognizing your gifts from God—
your attributes, your personality type, your lofty desires. Name them
and claim them every day. We are all created not just to be good but
to be great! We were created by our great God and destined to
be great. Don't settle for being a good parent; strive to be a great
parent. Don't strive to be a good neighbor; become a great neighbor.
Don't just be a good employee, be the best you can be by being great
at the work you do. Don't be a good Christian or Jew or Muslim;
be a great person who lives your faith each day. What is your next
step to becoming a great person? Think in terms of greatness, not
just success. Memorize this small prayer, write it on your bathroom
mirror, and repeat it often; it's powerful. It goes like this: "Help
me, Lord, to grow from good to great!" Don't sell yourself short.
God will help you develop into the truly great human being you
are meant to be.

Prayer

Lord, strengthen my belief in the strength of your love for me,
moving me from good to great! Amen.

God's Side

"If God is for us, who is against us?"—ROMANS 8:31

....

Concerning the Civil War, someone asked Abraham Lincoln if God was on his side. Lincoln replied: "Sir, my concern is not whether God is on our side. My greatest concern is to be on God's side. For God is always right." Lincoln was a wise man; he wanted to be right, as we all do. He was smart enough to see that the highest wisdom belongs to the highest Being: God. So he searched the Bible, understood the basic dignity and humanity of every person, and concluded that everyone, regardless of race, had inalienable rights from God. We all want God to be on our side, but first we need to be sure we're on God's side.

Prayer

Lord, remind me to read the Bible often to see if I'm on your side. Amen.

Defend the Absent Person

"Blessed are the peacemakers, for they will be called children of God."—MATTHEW 5:9

....

There's an old saying: "Defend the absent person." When you are in a group and the name of someone else comes up and criticism begins to creep into the conversation, be sure to be the first to "defend the absent person"—the one they are talking about. Do this for two reasons. First, it's an act of love—you took the high road. Secondly, others will learn to trust you—because they are thinking that when they are the absent person, you will defend them. People will respect and trust you! They know you may someday defend them. Who will that absent person be today?

Prayer

Lord, give me the courage to defend the absent person. Amen.

Be Sincere

"Let love be genuine."—ROMANS 12:9

....

Love has several definitions. I like the one by St. John Paul II: "Love is the sincere gift of oneself to another." Yes, it's the choice to give oneself to another. And it's a sincere gift. The word *sincere* comes from the two Latin words *sine* and *cera*. *Sine* means "without," and *cera* means "wax"—"without wax." Sculptors of marble statues used to cover up their mistakes with wax that looked like marble. It was fake. Sincere love is real love, true and transparent love. No hooks, no tricks—what you see is what you get. Make your love a sincere gift to another—real and from the heart.

Prayer

"Lord, help me to love as you love—with sincerity. Amen.

Race Ahead!

"I press on to make it my own, because Christ Jesus
has made me his own."—Philippians 3:12

Don't let the past hold you back from running the race before you
toward the ultimate goal—life with joy and community in heaven,
the eternal life of love fulfilled. Past mistakes, past sins, and past
disappointments can often form a daily dark cloud over our heads.
Pray to put all the past in your loving Father's healing hands. St.
Paul made huge mistakes. But after his conversion, he wrote to the
Philippians: "I do not consider that I have made it my own; but this
one thing I do: forgetting what lies behind and straining forward
to what lies ahead" (Philippians 3:13). Leave the dark clouds of the
past in the past. Run toward the bright light of God before you.

Prayer

Lord, help me keep that goal—you—clearly in sight! Amen.

Lasting Fruit

"I am the vine; you are the branches. Those who abide in me
and I in them bear much fruit, because apart from
me you can do nothing."—JOHN 15:5

Will what I do during my lifetime make any difference? Maybe in
the present, but what about years from now? Will the good fruit
of love and justice I have borne really last? Jesus gave us the answer
to that question: Yes! If our life is connected by faith, hope, and
love, we will bear "fruit that will last" (John 15:16). So you and I do
what we discern to be God's will for us in each moment; we do our
duties as best we can, and we do them as much as possible out of a
motive of love for God and others. God not only guarantees good,
nourishing fruit from our labors, but fruit that, by his power, will
last and nourish others in the years ahead.

Prayer

Lord, my life will make a difference now and in the future if I abide
in you. Amen.

Doing Good with God

"The harvest is plentiful, but the laborers are few;
therefore ask the Lord of the harvest to send out
laborers into his harvest."—LUKE:10:2

Have you ever planned to do a good deed and felt a little nervous? *Will others accept the good I'm trying to do? Will I be criticized? Will this good I want to do really be a benefit for anyone?* Not to worry—if we are doing the good deed with sincere love, then God inspired it within us. Therefore, God is not only with us—he goes before us. In fact, God is there ahead of us, waiting for us. Go for it! He's always there to create a positive outcome. Go there and go with confidence, with a smile on your face. God is waiting! Even if the results seem disappointing, he will draw good from it. You can't lose!

Prayer

Give me the love and courage to do the good you inspire me to do. Amen.

Act with Courage

"The Lord is my light and my salvation;
whom shall I fear?"—PSALM 27:1

St. John Paul II used to always encourage people: "Do not be afraid of anything." If we know there is something we must do, although it may be unpleasant or difficult, "do not be afraid of anything." If it is good and needed and will straighten out a situation, then "do not be afraid." Why? Because if it is true and good, you are doing God's work. God is there before you. Pray for courage and love and start out with God in faith. Pray that you will do what God wants you to do, no more and no less. God wants it done. Do not be afraid of anything. Do your part, and God will do his part. I love what John Wayne, the great cowboy icon, used to say when facing a difficult situation: "Be scared to death but saddle up anyway."

Prayer

This good thing may be difficult to do, but as St. Paul said, "I can do all things through him who strengthens me" (Philippians 4:13). Amen.

Everyday Fortitude

"Let us not grow weary in doing what is right."—GALATIANS 6:9

Of the four basic virtues (prudence, justice, fortitude, and temperance), fortitude (or courage) is the most difficult for many of us. Fortitude is exercised when someone does a heroic act, such as jumping into a flooded river basin to save a child. But the greatest exercise of fortitude is long-term—not just one heroic act, but the heroism of working hard each day to support oneself or others, daily caring for a sick parent or friend or physically challenged child. Perseverance is the real virtue of fortitude. It's a gift from God, so we must pray for it and use it.

Prayer

Lord, strengthen the virtue of courage within me. Thank you for the courage I do have. Amen.

Work with God

"I can do all things through him who
strengthens me."—PHILIPPIANS 4:13

There is a very wise saying: "Trust God in such a way that you do
not forget to do your part. But do your part in such a way that you
realize that God alone is at work." How true that when we begin
a project or a healthy relationship, we do our best, although the
results may not always be the best possible. But do it with God. Then
watch and see. You will be amazed. God's love is not only present
at this very moment, but all throughout this day. His loving, gentle
guidance has a plan for your day today. So prayerfully set good goals
for yourself. Then do what you can to peacefully accomplish them
one at a time, remembering that God is at work to create a fruitful
outcome. Be calm because you know his love is in charge, and he
is working his perfect plan through you and for you. His Spirit is
making you strong, loving, and wise. Let your work be inspired by
the Holy Spirit. Remember, God often writes straight with crooked
lines. If the lines look a little crooked, trust even more and see how
God will make them straight. He is loving and powerful. Do your
best peacefully and well, trusting in God's providence. It is going to
work out better than you think!

Prayer

Lord, you want to partner with me on life's journey. Help me to do
my part well and trust you for the rest. Amen.

God Is Your Partner

"In all your ways acknowledge him,
and he will make straight your paths."—PROVERBS 3:6

Living well is a process of self-discipline! Self-discipline is like dancing with another person—you must know your partner. We humans all have the same wonderful partner, the one who created us, our loving, compassionate God! The discipline is to trust God's gentle guidance. Try to pray about everything you do and leave the outcome to him. Do not fear God's loving will. Remember that he loves you and wants you to dance well—and to enjoy the dance! God only wants your happiness. God only wants what is best for you and me. The more we trust his guidance, the more quickly and easily God guides our steps. Trust in God's wisdom and God's ways, and the dance will be a real adventure! A wonderful adventure!

Prayer

Lord, thank you for choosing me to be your partner. Amen.

God's Plan

"I cry to God Most High, to God who fulfills his
purpose for me."—PSALM 57:2

....

Through the prophet Jeremiah, we hear comforting words addressed
to each of us personally: "For surely I know the plans I have for you,
says the Lord—plans for your welfare and not for harm, to give you
a future with hope" (Jeremiah 29:11). That's right! In his great love,
our God has not only created you in your mother's womb, but he
has a plan—a great plan—for your greatness. He can do nothing
less for us. Take a moment of silent prayer sometime today and ask
God to enlighten you with his plan for your whole life—as well as
for today—and trust it. If you persevere in asking, God will gladly
reveal it to you. Read the Bible prayerfully. Your faith and your good
reasoning will put the pieces of the puzzle together.

Prayer

Lord, you have created me for a purpose. Help me to cooperate
with your plan. Amen.

Only God Can Judge Rightly

"Do not judge, so that you may not be judged."—MATTHEW 7:1

Our human intelligence makes it impossible not to judge. We make judgments all the time—about the weather, the clothes we wear, and the TV shows we watch. But what is the best way to interpret someone else's behavior? Maybe someone in your family or a neighbor or a work associate did or said something hurtful or puzzling to you. The best approach is to remember one thing: You don't know everything behind that behavior. It's like a puzzle: you don't see the whole picture until all the pieces are in place. You know some of the pieces, but not all of them. Give the best interpretation to the unknown pieces behind the behavior.

A holy priest once said: "Your kinder judgments are your better ones." Let your assumptions be kind. Assume the best. Make excuses for others. You probably will be right. Your kinder judgments will most of the time be your better ones. You'll probably be more at peace yourself. Be content with the fact that you just don't have all the facts. Give the other person the benefit of the doubt. Assume the best. You probably will be right. And you will live a more peaceful life.

Prayer

Lord, soften my heart and sharpen my reason when judging someone's behavior. Remind me that I can't judge the motives of others—only you can see into someone's heart. Amen.

See the Good News

"[Love] bears all things, believes all things, hopes all things, endures all things."—1 CORINTHIANS 13:7

....

Unfortunately, people often rub us the wrong way. Their faults seem more obvious than their virtues. It's so easy to focus on another's shortcomings, faults, failures, sins, and defects. It takes love to focus on another's good qualities and virtues, not denying their shortcomings but focusing your attention on their good qualities. The decision to go positive is called love. It's a choice and is often followed by a feeling of empathy for that person. And that's how you and I can love. It begins by focusing on another's good qualities. They are there—just look for them.

Try to see the good news in another person. Sure, the bad news is obvious to us. But the good news is just as real. It's there. Try to think about it—focus on it. Comment to others about it. That helps them and you. That's how to grow positive relationships! You'll probably be a happier person yourself, realizing that the positive aspects of another's personality are just as real as the negative. That's the truth.

Prayer

Lord, you see the good news in each of us. Help me to see the good news in others. Amen.

Whose Problem?

"But the wisdom from above is first pure, then peaceable, gentle, willing to yield, full of mercy."—JAMES 3:17

Almost every day we experience a conflict with someone else. It may be major or very minor. It's good to step back and ask yourself this question: "Whose problem is this?" Sometimes the problem might be yours. Often it is not. And that's when you calm down and say to yourself, "Not my problem!" Of course we can wonder what the other person's problem is. But we really don't know. There's a good chance that person doesn't know either. Whisper a prayer to the Lord for the wisdom to know whose problem it really is. If the problem is yours, then own it. If it's the other person's, offer a prayer for him or her to face and solve it. That's true wisdom!

Prayer

Lord, grant me the gift of right judgment and insight in conflict situations. Amen.

Don't Flunk Life!

"You will know the truth, and the truth
will make you free"—JOHN 8:32

Don't flunk life! How does one flunk life? Anyone can flunk if we get the wrong answers to the four big questions of life:

Where did I come from?

Who am I?

Where am I going?

How do I get there?

The answers are simple. God himself gives us the answers to each of these four questions in the Scriptures:

I was created by God.

I am made in God's image and likeness, as a human person with intelligence and free will.

God has a beautiful, joyous eternal home for me in heaven beyond this life.

I get there by walking in the steps God has shown us in his Son, Jesus Christ, outlined in the New Testament.

Get the right answers to the four big questions and you won't flunk life. You'll pass with flying colors.

Prayer

Help me to reflect on the big four questions and get the right answers to them. Amen.

God Is in Charge

"The Lord is on my side to help me."—PSALM 118:7

....

Maybe you've decided on a course of action for the week. If that plan is in line with God's will, nothing can stop you from making it happen. You may well encounter obstacles, but don't give up— don't get discouraged. If it's in God's will, nothing can stop it. Do not expect everything to be easy. But do expect God's help. Remember, he is at your side. Be sure to let everything unfold gradually according to his Providence. God is in charge of time. He invented it! Let him set the pace. Simply ask God to show you the pace, moment by moment. Walk with courage and trust, and all will turn out supremely well. The more we trust in our loving Father, the more easily and quickly God works everything out.

Prayer

Lord, help me to see your loving Providence in everything. Amen.

Develop Each Cardinal Virtue

"For this very reason, you must make every effort to
support your faith with goodness, and goodness
with knowledge."—2 PETER 1:5

The Greek philosophers outlined four basic strengths of character, and these are also found in the Hebrew and Christian Scriptures; they are the four cardinal virtues of prudence, justice, fortitude, and temperance. Some modern theologians suggest that we might restate these four with simple virtues: faith, hope, and love. Be humble, be hospitable, be merciful, be faithful, be forgiving, be vigilant, and be reliable. Such virtues develop best if focused on one at a time. Strengthening one of these helps to develop the rest. Focus on one virtue today or this week. Think about that one. Pray for the strength you'll need and practice it often.

Prayer

Lord, give me the patience I need with myself as I work to develop these cardinal virtues. Amen.

Be Prudent

"It is the wisdom of the clever to understand
where they go."—PROVERBS 14:8

The Book of Wisdom in the Old Testament teaches that a wise person is one who is developing the four character habits. One of those habits is prudence. The wise person is the truly prudent person. Prudence is the habit that enables us to recognize in any situation what is good and what is evil, what is right and what is wrong. Also, the prudent person has a correct knowledge of things that ought to be done and things that should be avoided. If you are prudent, you usually first take counsel with yourself and then with others. Finally, you judge on the basis of the evidence at hand, and then act on that knowledge. Do this often, even daily, and you will continue to grow into a truly wise and prudent person.

Prayer

Lord, help me to be prudent, to see situations as you see them. Amen.

Temper Justice with Mercy

"If anyone is detected in a transgression, you who have
received the Spirit should restore such a one in a
spirit of gentleness."—GALATIANS 6:1

As one of the four cardinal virtues, justice is a character habit developed as one chooses to give to everyone what is really due to them. The main goal of justice is respecting the rights of others, especially if I owe someone something, or when I choose to respect someone's natural rights, such as the right to educate one's children or one's legal and civil rights. As you choose to give everyone his or her rightful due, you are developing the character trait of a just person. You are a just person!

We must carefully consider what the just thing really is in every situation. As a legislative leader and president, Abraham Lincoln realized the power of compassion and mercy. He once noted, "I have always found that mercy bears richer fruits than strict justice." People will respond more positively when justice is tempered with mercy. Their behavior is more likely to improve. Yes, we need justice, but it needs to be tempered by mercy whenever possible.

Prayer

Lord, sharpen my powers of reason to truly see what the just thing is in every situation. And help us all to temper justice with mercy. Amen.

Be Moderate

"Do not be conformed to this world, but be transformed
by the renewing of your minds."—ROMANS 12:2

....

A person with a strong character has usually developed the virtue of temperance or moderation, one of the four cardinal, or basic human, virtues. Moderation means balance, and it's difficult because the pleasures of life are easily overindulged in. Developing moderation means that I enjoy the good things of life, the pleasures of life, but remain free, not letting them control or dominate me. Really, the more one is free of them, the more one actually enjoys them. Living in moderation creates strength in one's character. Neither too much nor too little—that's the virtue of moderation. In Latin, the philosophers taught: *In medio stat Virtus.* Virtue is in the center, not too little or too much of anything. That's temperance.

Prayer

Lord, help me to walk in the middle of the road, enjoying your gifts—not too much, not too little. Amen.

Building Character

"As he who called you is holy, be holy yourselves in
all your conduct."—1 PETER 1:15

Have you ever heard the axiom "We are our own parents"? It simply
means that we give birth to our own character, or personhood. And
we do so by what we choose to do or not do: our free will. I make
myself by what I choose. For example, if I choose to steal, it's not
just an act of theft. I become a thief. I make myself a different
person, a thief. Or if I help the needy, I don't merely do something
good for someone; I become a charitable person. Yes, in a way we
are our own parents. We create ourselves by the choices we make.
What are you choosing? That is what you are becoming.

Prayer

Lord, help me to see each choice I make today as an opportunity to
grow into the person you are creating me to be. Amen.

Answer God's Call with Faith

"For truly, I tell you, if you have faith the size of a
mustard seed, you will say to this mountain, 'Move from
here to there', and it will move; and nothing will be
impossible for you."—MATTHEW 17:20

A real leader once said, "Do not wait for leaders—just do it alone,
person to person." Mother Teresa did it alone, as she saw hungry,
sick, and dying men, women, and children in the back alleys and the
inner city of Calcutta, India. She left the secure convent where she
lived with other nuns to reach out to those on the street. She did
not wait for the government or a social leader to pave the way. Her
selfless example soon attracted dozens of young women, and they
became the Missionaries of Charity, an order that now ministers in
practically every country in the world.

Prayer

Lord, give me the courage to act when you call and the faith to
know that nothing is impossible for you. Amen.

Your Mission

"Jesus said to them again, 'Peace be with you. As the
Father has sent me, so I send you.'"—JOHN 20:21

Each of us has a mission in life. Yes, you and I have a mission.
The word *mission* comes from the Latin word *missio*, which means
"sent." So you and I are not just born into this world; we are sent by
the One who created us as persons, in our mother's womb, giving
us intelligence and a free will. But how do we know our mission,
our purpose, here and now? One way is simply to accept where my
life is right now. I'm here in this place, this time, this situation. Yes,
God's loving Providence has placed me here. I may be at work, or
married, or single, or in a hospital bed, or in pain or joy.

Your mission in life at this time may be obvious. If so, pursue
it peacefully with God's help. If you are unsure, ask your loving
Creator to gently reveal it to you. If you're still not sure, then
consider what you think it might be. Pray for God's wisdom, and
you will know. Ask, and you shall receive. Do what is right; do your
best and do it peacefully and confidently. In God's plan you are
necessary for this world. You are on mission right now. Work to
accomplish it with God's help.

Prayer

Lord, help me to see my mission in life as it unfolds before me.
I pray that one day we will say together, "Mission accomplished!"
Amen.

My Purpose

"I cry to God Most High, to God who fulfills his
purpose for me."—Psalm 57:2

We are all impressed by the heroes of history, but I'm especially
impressed by the great heroines. Take, for example, the nineteen-
year-old French woman Joan of Arc, a fifteenth-century leader of
the French army. She successfully led her troops by the words and
visions she received from St. Michael the Archangel, St. Margaret,
and St. Catherine. She was captured in 1430 and sold to the
English. Because she wore a man's soldier uniform and had visions,
she was condemned as a heretic to be burned at the stake. Her
final words were: "God is with me. I am not afraid; I was born for
this." This nineteen-year-old maiden and mystic knew her purpose
in life. God will show us ours if we ask.

Prayer

Lord, show me what I was born for, my purpose. Amen.

Your Mission Statement

"Let the wise also hear and gain in learning."—PROVERBS 1:5

Steven Covey, renowned management consultant, is the author of the book *The Seven Habits of Highly Successful People.* The first of his seven habits is simple: "Begin with the end in mind." Begin with a picture of the end of your life as your frame of reference by which all your choices are examined. By keeping that end, that ultimate goal, before you, you can be certain that whatever you do on a particular day does not violate that goal. Each day should contribute to your final goal. I suggest that the best goal is beyond this short earthly life. It's life beyond this world, living the unconditional love of God and others in another space called heaven. Begin each day with that end in mind—your true eternal home.

Covey goes on to suggest that you should write down your personal mission statement. In the first grade, I memorized my goal in life from the penny catechism: "To know, love, and serve God in this life and to be happy with him forever in the next." After these many years, that's still true. My mission statement guides me in how to love: love God, love neighbor, love myself. Place love at the center of your mission statement. It's the high road, worthy of each of us. And it goes in the right direction.

Prayer

Lord, let my mission statement be the same as your mission statement is for me. Amen.

Success through Humility

"Do nothing from selfishness ambition or conceit, but in humility regard others as better than yourselves."—PHILIPPIANS 2:3

If you study the lives of successful leaders, they all seem to have one common characteristic or virtue: humility. For example, Andrew Carnegie's tombstone reads: "Here lies a man who knew how to enlist in his service better men than himself." Humility is knowing the truth about yourself, the positive and the negative, embracing both and acting on it. Because he truthfully faced and owned his own weaknesses, Carnegie found others who could compensate with their strengths.

I recently heard a presentation by Vern Dosch, founder of the NISC software giant. His principles for success in business were quite simple: "First, always do the right thing; if it's not the right thing, don't do it. It will eventually backfire on you. Second, tell the truth. People will learn to trust you. Third, be humble with a warm spirit. Finally, be courageous in always doing the right thing, in always telling the truth, and in being a humble person. You will be a success, and you will become a successful human being."

Prayer

Lord, grant me the grace of a humble heart so that I may embrace my weaknesses and, like St. Paul, empty myself of the pride of self-sufficiency so your power can work through me to do your will in this world. Amen.

God's Light from Holy Scripture

"Truthful lips endure forever, but a lying tongue
lasts only a moment."—PROVERBS 12:19

Abraham Lincoln has left us with some profound words of wisdom, words that showed us his solid character. He once wrote, "I am not bound to win, but I am bound to be true. I am not bound to succeed, but I am bound to live by the light that I have." Lincoln would not have been swayed by what might have been politically correct. He had to be true to the light of the basic truths of his faith. Lincoln read the deeper truths about humanity as he meditated on the words he read in the Bible. He welcomed those lights that formed his character. In the long run, he was a success because he was true to the lights God gave him.

Prayer

Lead me, Lord, in the light of truth and teach me your ways. Amen.

Time, Words, and Opportunities

"Conduct yourself wisely toward outsiders, making the most of the time. Let your speech always be gracious, seasoned with salt, so that you may know how you ought to answer everyone."—COLOSSIANS 4:5–6

What are the things we never get back? I suggest these are the Big Three: time, words, and opportunities. Once they're gone, they're gone. So, we must be careful not to take time for granted. Don't waste it. It is running out, so use it wisely. Use words wisely as well. Once they are out of your mouth, you can't take them back. Also, watch for the opportunities God's Providence puts in your path. Don't let them pass you by. Be courageous, do your part, and let God do the rest.

Prayer

Lord, help me to see your hand in all things and to use time, words, and opportunities well and wisely. Amen.

The Learning Curve of Life

"You must understand this, my beloved: let everyone be quick to listen, slow to speak, slow to anger."—JAMES 1:19

Life is a huge learning curve. To stop learning is to stop living. This holds true for leaders, especially leaders in the home, at work, or in social groups. It is said that the best leaders are the best listeners. Each of us is, in some way, a leader to others. We must be slow to speak, quick to listen, and patient in developing our thoughts. We often ask our children, "What did you learn today?" We encourage them to listen. How about you and me? What did you and I learn today or yesterday? Were we listening? The best leaders are the best listeners.

Prayer

Almighty Father, open my ears; help me to be a good listener. Amen.

God's Business Model

"So, if I, your Lord and Teacher, have washed your feet,
you also ought to wash one another's feet."—JOHN 13:14

I recently heard a lecture by Vern Dosch, founder of NISC and author of the book *Wired Differently*. He preaches and practices servant leadership, and that is the key to the success of his business. Being "wired differently" is the opposite of the dog-eat-dog approach to business. Dosch writes that in a servant leadership culture, we learn by choice and by example that if we want to be great, we have to serve others respectfully. He truly respected his employees, and they respected him. The by-product was an immensely profitable business.

You and I experience leadership all the time. Either we are in a leadership position in the family, at work, in our community, or we are under the leadership of someone else, in government, at work, at church, or in society. Servant leaders share their power, put the needs of their employees first, and help them develop themselves in achieving organizational success. If you're a leader, be a servant leader. You'll achieve your goals and in the process, develop the people who help you get there. Servant leadership works for families, organizations, and businesses. Try it!

Prayer

Lord, grant me grace to live out my vocation to be just to your people, and to be a true servant to them. Amen.

Be a Leader

"Whoever wishes to be great among you must be
your servant."—MATTHEW 20:26

....

Whether we are aware of it or not, each one of us in some small way—or maybe a major way—is a leader to others. President John Quincy Adams once said, "If your actions inspire others to dream more, learn more, and become more, you are a leader." Perhaps you are a leader in your workplace. Certainly in your family you are a leader, looked up to by your children, younger siblings, or cousins. Unknowingly we are often leaders to our peers by our faith in God, our charity, or our patience. Others notice these qualities in us and feel inspired to learn more, to dream more, and to become more. Don't sell yourself short. In some way you are a leader to others. Who might those people be in your life? Lead them!

Prayer

Show me, Lord, where I am a leader. Help me to lead by serving. Amen.

Real Confidence

"But if we hope for what we do not see, we wait
for it with patience."—ROMANS 8:25

Start your day with hope, confidence, and trust in the One who unconditionally and irrevocably loves and cares for you, our loving God who reveals himself as a tender, caring, omnipresent Father. Trust the love God has for you. It's real and it's there today for you. Believe in him and his love, and you will grow in peace because you are becoming a person of hope anchored in the One who will always come through for you. As one of the saints wrote, "Faith brings what seemed hopeless within our reach." Is there something that seems hopeless to you? Have faith in God's power and love. What seems hopeless is now within your reach.

Prayer

Lord, help me to trust in your loving, caring, powerful hand. Amen.

Acquire Wisdom

"If any of you is lacking in wisdom, ask God,
who gives to all generously and ungrudgingly,
and it will be given you."—JAMES 1:5

....

We all have knowledge, but do we possess wisdom? Do we use our knowledge to create a better world or to create positive relationships? That's wisdom. So, what is the source of wisdom? Solomon was known for his great wisdom, presumably the wisest man who ever lived. At twelve years of age, the young man suddenly became the new king of Israel. God spoke to the boy at night and invited him to ask for whatever he wanted. He replied, "I want wisdom," and it was richly granted to him. God has wisdom and readily gives wisdom to those who ask for it. Do what Solomon did. Ask for wisdom—every day—and you will receive it. Our world needs wisdom—your wisdom!

Prayer

Lord, please give me the gift of wisdom. Amen.

Think First

"A gentle tongue is a tree of life."—PROVERBS 15:4

I enjoy reading the Wisdom books of the Hebrews Scriptures. The sayings have proven true for countless generations. In the Book of Sirach, for example, we are counseled to think before we speak. It counsels, "Be consistent in your thoughts, steadfast in your words; be swift to hear, but slow to answer." Remember the advice, "Once you have said it, you can't take it back." So before saying something ask yourself if you would be proud to have it posted on social media. If it's something you might regret, keep it to yourself. The wise person is the one who thinks first before speaking. The Book of Proverbs says it in a positive way: "The right word at the right time is the precious gold set in silver!"

Prayer

Lord, help me to say the right thing at the right time. Amen.

Speak Up Gently

"Well meant are the wounds a friend inflicts."—PROVERBS 27:6

It's usually difficult and often uncomfortable to discuss the key and often important issues that face us today. Rather than alienate people, our tendency is to keep our opinions to ourselves. The sad thing is that our opinion might be just the insight the other person needs. And if expressed with a measure of gentleness and respect, it could be helpful to him or her. It's important, in the right setting, to share our insights and positions. It's important for one's own integrity. Martin Luther King Jr. once warned, "Our lives begin to end the day we become silent on things that matter." Be prudent, but don't be silent. Speak gently and respectfully. Don't be silent on the things that matter.

Prayer

Lord, give me courage and a gentle spirit when I speak. Amen.

Love Your Enemy

"Do not be overcome by evil, but overcome
evil with good."—ROMANS 12:21

When we are wronged, we naturally want to retaliate. That emotional response is almost immediate. But retaliation often makes things worse. The Old Testament taught fairness: "An eye for an eye; a tooth for a tooth." But Jesus taught the way of inner peace, and emotional restraint: "Love your enemy; do good to those who persecute you." Centuries later Gandhi taught the same thing. "Whenever you are confronted with an opponent, conquer him or her with love." And St. Paul taught, "Do not be overcome by evil, but overcome evil with good." Hard to do, but it results in peace. Think about something good you can do for the person who has wronged you. It works. It really does.

Prayer

Lord, help me when I feel overcome with evil. Help me to counter that with good. Amen.

New Open Doors

"The word of the Lord came to Jonah
a second time."—JONAH 3:1

Alexander Graham Bell often failed in his dream to create electronic vocal communications, but he was an incurable optimist. He once wrote, "When one door closes, another door opens, but we so often look so long and so respectfully upon the closed door that we do not see the ones which open for us." As I look at my own journey of life, I am grateful for the doors that were closed because I now see some of the doors that were opened for me. Don't look at the closed door; that's a waste of time! Look for the ones opening in front of you. They are there! Don't be afraid to walk through them.

Prayer

Lord, give me the faith and trust in you to see and walk through the new doors you open before me. Amen.

Your Daring Adventure

"I will strengthen you, I will help you, I will uphold you
with my victorious right hand."—ISAIAH 41:10

Helen Keller was one of the most successful women in American history. At nineteen months of age, she lost her sight and hearing. She learned to speak, overcome her disabilities, and graduate from two colleges. She once wrote: "One's character cannot be developed in ease and quiet. Only through the experience of trial and suffering can the soul be strengthened. Life is either a daring adventure or nothing." What is your daring adventure? Think it over. Write it down. Share it with someone, pray for courage, and then go for it! "Life is either a daring adventure or nothing."

Prayer

Lord, show me my daring adventure now and lead me through it. Amen.

Good Listeners

"Let everyone be quick to listen, slow to speak,
slow to anger."—JAMES 1:19

We all could use a brief course in how to listen. As our listening skills become better, we not only know better what to say to others, we also develop the wisdom to know when it's better to say nothing at all. Good listening skills automatically make us much more open, present, and responsive to others. You may have noticed the special sincerity in people whom you know are good listeners.

I suggest three key attitudes as you listen to other people. First, let your own interest in those people be apparent to them. They can sense whether or not you care. Second, as you listen, try to sense the feeling behind what the other person is saying. Third, don't be thinking about what you're going to say. You might simply feed back to him or her what you just heard said. You may have a question or two. Now you are really listening. They know it, they feel valued, and they will appreciate you.

Finally, let your mantra be, "Listen longer." When someone else is talking or disagreeing with us, our brain already has the answer or objection. We know what we are going to say. But hold it for few seconds—listen longer. Often that person will surprise you with his or her next thought.

Prayer

Lord, help me to realize that careful listening is genuine loving. Amen.

Morality

"The good person brings good things out of a good treasure,
and the evil person brings evil things out of an
evil treasure."—MATTHEW 12:35

Here's something we all wonder about. How do I know if something is right or wrong? Is it a matter of feeling or thinking? If I think or feel something is right or wrong, does that make it right or wrong? But people differ according to their feelings. There is a simple way we can all agree on whether something is right—it's right if it helps me or others. Something is wrong if it hurts me or others. If it really builds up and helps, then it's right. If it hurts me or someone else, then it's wrong. This little moral compass helps us when discussing or thinking about what is right and what is wrong.

Prayer

Lord, help me to be keenly aware of those things that hurt and those that help. Give me the courage to choose the latter. Amen.

In the Present

"So do not worry about tomorrow, for tomorrow will bring worries of its own. Today's trouble is enough for today."—MATTHEW 6:34

....

Live today well. Remember that God only asks us to do one thing at a time, never two. It doesn't matter if the job is making a bed or delivering a commencement address at a graduation. We should strive to put our heart into it, do it simply, and give it our best effort. Live in the present moment. We shouldn't try to solve more than one problem at a time. That habit of focus will significantly reduce the stress we bring upon ourselves. Yes, live in the NOW, in the present moment. Trust in God who is interested in you and loves you. Let God handle what only God can handle: the past and the future. One thing at a time, that's the way to live.

Prayer

Lord, help me to see that my responsibility is in the present moment. The past and the future are yours. Amen.

Live Today Fully

"I give you a new commandment, that you love
one another."—John 13:34

This day is a new day. It has never been before, and it will not exist again. Make today the best day you've ever lived. The key to making this a successful day is simply *love*. When we love, we are at our best. We are created by God out of his love. Our destiny is eternal love, and eternal love begins when we freely choose to be other-centered. Begin by choosing to think positively, to think of serving others, to think love. Then choose to do small, loving things for others. That will make today the best day you've ever lived. As Mother Teresa said: "Do little things with great love." You will be a better person, others will be better, and the world will be better.

Prayer

Lord, help me to realize that my gestures of love make this a better world. Amen.

Reputation versus Reality

"And whenever you pray, do not be like the hypocrites; for they love to stand and pray in the synagogues and at the street corners, so that they may be seen by others. Truly I tell you, they have received their reward."—MATTHEW 6:5

I love some of Abraham Lincoln's sayings. He had great insight into human nature. He once wrote, "Character is like a tree, and reputation is its shadow. The shadow is what we think it is, but the tree is the real thing." In other words, what people think of you or me, our reputation, is just the shadow of our true character. Hopefully you and I have good reputations. Our duty is to make sure that a good reputation truly reflects the good character within us. That's something we have to keep developing.

Prayer

Lord, help me to develop a good reputation that reflects my true character. Amen.

Build Others Up

"How can you say to your neighbor, 'Let me take the speck out of your eye,' while the log is in your own eye?... You hypocrite, first take the log out of your own eye, and then you will see clearly to take the speck out of your neighbor's eye."—MATTHEW 7:4–5

Because we are human beings with strengths and weaknesses, virtues and vices, it is easy to spot another's weakness or vices or be critical of his or her decisions. Abraham Lincoln said that "the only person who has the right to criticize is the one who has the heart to help." President Lincoln challenged each of us to love—to have a heart of compassion for the one we criticize. If I am critical, then how can I be helpful? My criticism is only helpful if my heart is ready to help. The name for that is "constructive criticism." It suggests a better path that benefits everyone. I should hesitate to tear down unless I am ready to build up. That positive attitude always makes the situation better.

Prayer

Lord, when I feel myself becoming critical of another, help me to think instead how I can be helpful to that person. Amen.

The Power in Kind Words

"Pleasant words are like a honeycomb, sweetness to the soul
and health to the body."—PROVERBS 16:24

Have you ever reflected on the good feeling you get when someone says a kind word to you? Words are powerful. And kind words seem to have an endless echo within us. They change us. They build us up! Mother Teresa spread kind words to others whenever possible. She said, "Kind words can be short and easy, but their echoes are truly endless; this is because their echoes are echoes of love, and love builds us up." So be a builder. Build others up! We can all do that! Love others with sincere words of kindness. We will never know all the good that our kind words accomplish in the lives of other people. Blaise Pascal wrote: "Kind words do not cost much. Yet they accomplish much."

Prayer

Lord, fill my heart with love and fill my words with kindness. Amen.

Growth in Maturity

"When I became an adult, I put an end
to childish ways."—1 CORINTHIANS 13:11

The Maturity Continuum is a gradual movement from dependence to independence to interdependence. We need to avoid judging everything by dependence—it's always someone else's fault—"you didn't take care of me," or "you didn't come through." It's always "you." Independence is next. It's the paradigm of the "I": "I can do it"; "I am responsible"; "I am self-reliant." Finally, interdependence: the paradigm of *we*. "We can do it"; "we can cooperate"; and "we can combine our talents and abilities and create something greater together." If we keep the *you* and *I* paradigms at a minimum and strive for the *we* approach, our efforts to be effective will pay much bigger dividends. Try to think today of the "we" approach to life.

Prayer

Lord, your plan is for us to work together, as you work together as Father, Son, and Holy Spirit. Amen.

Self-Control

"Like a city breached , without walls,
is one who lacks self-control."—PROVERBS 25:28

....

How can I change the world around me for the better? Good question! The great spiritual leader in India, Mahatma Gandhi, often counseled: "Be the change you wish to see in the world." He was truly a wise man. The change I hope for must begin with me—not outside myself. Gandhi also noted: "An ounce of patience is worth more than a ton of preaching." Patience is a virtue within oneself. Gandhi saw the fruit of the virtues in his own life. He was convinced that "in a gentle way you can shake the world." And shake the world he did.

Prayer

Lord, help me to see that there is nothing stronger than gentleness, and nothing is more gentle than real strength. Amen.

America's Greatness

"The name of the Lord is a strong tower;
the righteous run into it and are safe."—PROVERBS 18:10

....

Alexis de Tocqueville, the nineteenth-century French diplomat, identified the strengths and weaknesses of the new "American Experiment." He wrote that "the greatness of America is not in being more enlightened than any other nation, but rather in her ability to recognize her faults." Many are concerned about the situation our nation finds itself in today.

George Washington would have placed our future in the hands of Divine Providence. During the Revolutionary War, in March 1781 he wrote to William Gordon, "We have, as you very justly observe, abundant reason to thank Providence for its many favorable interpositions in our behalf. It has at times been my only dependence, for all other resources seemed to have failed us."

Dr. Martin Luther King Jr. once said, "We Americans must learn to live together as brothers and sisters, or we will perish together as fools." Our survival is determined by our willingness to accept one another. That is the greatness of America.

Prayer

Lord, as a nation, help us to desire righteousness over rights and sacrifice over selfishness. Help me to make our country great by reaching out to join hands with others. Amen.

Jesus Needs Our Help

"For it is God who is at work in you, enabling you both to will and to work for his good pleasure."—PHILIPPIANS 2:13

I love the story in the Gospel of St. John of Jesus changing water into wine. I like it because Jesus performed a miracle to help a young, newly married couple whose wedding reception was short on wine, but also because he would not have done it without the help of the waiters who filled up the six stone jars with water. Jesus wanted and needed human cooperation to perform his first miracle. It is the same with us. He needs our participation to perform some of his miracles. Today he needs our prayers and good words to inspire and help others. He needs our good example to inspire the hearts of others. He needs our love to ignite love in the hearts of our family and friends. Like the wedding feast of Cana, he will perform the miracle, but he needs our cooperation. How can you participate in a miracle he wants to perform through you in the life of someone you know?

Prayer

Lord, help me to see how you can and do work through me. Amen.

Acknowledgments

....

This book with its numerous parts would never have been composed without the timeless efforts of my secretary, Michelle Miller.

I am grateful to my niece, Anna Correlli, who helped in the editing of several of these pages.

I am most grateful to Carolyn Lawrence who invited me to create one-minute "Thought of the Day" television productions in 2015, and continues to engage Channel 13/NBC with ongoing production. These pages are several of the TV spots.

I am most grateful to Don and Charlene Lamberti who have been the key supporters of this television outreach to inspire our central Iowa community.

I am thankful to the Bishop of the Des Moines diocese, Most Rev. William Joensen, PhD, for composing the Foreword to this book.

Finally, I am thankful to family and friends who have accompanied me on this journey with their encouragement and prayers.

About the Author

Monsignor Frank Bognanno, a retired priest in the Diocese of Des Moines, has faithfully served the Church for fifty-six years in a variety of positions including: pastor, associate pastor, chancellor, Moderator of the Curia, director of renewal, founder of the Emmaus Spirituality Program for Priests, author of *Contemplating Priestly Spirituality*, host of weekly programs for EWTN (1981-1990), creator of twenty-four RCIA instructional videos, lectures on Theology for Catechists at Franciscan University in Steubenville (2008-2016), Doctor of Ministry (D.Min) 1980, Iowa Board of Medicine member and fellow (2012-2015), coordinator of St. Pope John Paul II's 1979 visit to Iowa, current chaplain for Des Moines Legatus and chaplain for the Knights of Malta, and a member of the Knights of the Holy Sepulchre. He also serves as the spiritual director of the biennial Christ Our Life Catholic International Conference.